"You, follow me."

John 21:22

COME, HOLY SPIRIT: A DAILY DISCIPLESHIP TRAVEL LOG
FOR EASTER TO PENTECOST.

"YOU, FOLLOW ME"
VOLUME 4

© 2021 Justin Rossow and Next Step Press
ISBN: 9798723508255 · Imprint: Independently published

By Justin Rossow
Foreword by Leopoldo A. Sánchez M.
Series Editor, Justin Rossow

Some of the prayers include wording originally created by Justin Rossow and Leopoldo Sánchez for use in worship at St. Luke Lutheran Church, Ann Arbor, Michigan. Used by permission.

The Ripple Prayer originally created for *Ponder Anew: A Hymn Journal of Trust and Confidence.* Artwork © 2020 Valerie Matyas and Next Step Press. Used by permission.

The devotions for Day 12, Holding onto God's Delight and Day 33, God Delights in Play are both adapted from *Delight! Discipleship as the Adventure of Loving and Being Loved.* © 2020 Justin Rossow and Next Step Press. Used by permission.

Cover image: Clem Onojeghuo, unsplash.com/photos/hAhInPdviCk.

Special thanks to Valerie Matyas, Visual Faith™ Ministry's Educational Development Consultant, for content conversations; to Brett Jordan for cover design; to Deanna Rossow and Ellen Davis for proofreading; and to Leo Sánchez for *teología en conjuncto.* God has abundantly blessed you, my friends, and you have shared the overflow of that blessing with me. Thank you.

Inquiries or comments may be directed to
Curator@findmynextstep.org.

We help you take a next step

"You, follow me."
Volume Four

Come, Holy Spirit

A daily
discipleship travel log
for Easter to Pentecost

Justin Rossow

Introduction to the Series

"You, Follow Me!"

The series title comes from Jesus' invitation to Peter not only at the very beginning of the Gospels, but at the very end: the resurrected Jesus at the seashore extends a discipleship invitation to Peter again, even after Peter denied Jesus and ran away.

That invitation is for you, too: no matter how often you let Jesus down when push comes to shove, the resurrected Jesus wants to focus your eyes on what's important: "You, follow me!"

Why a "Discipleship Travel Log?"

Discipleship, at its core, is a journey: a journey of faith. Jesus invited his first disciples to "Come and see," and gave the command, "Follow me!"

This "travel log" is designed to help you pay attention to where Jesus is headed. It also gives you a way of tracking where you have been.

Because every faith journey has not only common destinations but unique twists and turns, you'll also find some new tools to explore. These discipling experiments are designed to help you follow Jesus in your everyday life.

If you can't see immediate progress or none of the new tools seem to help right away, don't give up! Following Jesus happens one step at a time.

A Journey for One (or More)

We follow Jesus better when we follow him together. In order to consistently take small next steps following Jesus, you need other people on your rope; people connected to the journey and to you.

And sometimes it's good and helpful to spend some time in single player mode.

Even Jesus, who had his large group gatherings, his small group of 12, and his micro-small group of three—even Jesus regularly went off by himself to pray. He needed the support of Peter, James, and John; he loved his interaction with the Twelve. But sometimes he needed to be alone with the Father and filled with the Spirit. Sometimes you need that, too.

So take some time with Jesus by yourself in this season. Or find a couple of friends to travel with you. Either way, Jesus promises to show up.

Volume 4: Easter to Pentecost

You can take this 40-day journey any time during the year. Right now, today, is always a good time to learn more about the Spirit and grow in dependence on Jesus.

And the time between Easter and Pentecost seems to resonate in a beautiful way with the Scripture, prayers, and Faith Experiments in this Discipleship Travel Log.

The work of Jesus finds a natural culmination in the events of Good Friday and Easter, and the work of the Spirit is on unique display at Pentecost. If you start Day 1 of this journey on one of the Saturdays after Easter, Day 40 will come right around Pentecost Sunday. Start whenever you are ready; or set aside special time after Easter: either way, the Spirit promises to be present and active in your life.

Foreword to Volume 4

Come, Holy Spirit!

How often have you prayed to the Holy Spirit? How regularly do you ask the Holy Spirit to come down, do his works in you, or fill you with his gifts?

We are more used to addressing Jesus and his Father in prayer, with good biblical precedent. From the earliest days of the church, prayers to the Lord Jesus and God the Father have been common in Christian devotion.

Often remembered as the first Christian martyr, St. Stephen prays to Jesus as he is being stoned by an enraged crowd: "*Lord, Jesus, receive my spirit…. Lord, do not hold this sin against them*" (Acts 7:59–60).

Here Stephen embodies his Lord Jesus' own prayers to the Father on the cross: "*Father, forgive them, for they do not know what they do…. Father, into your hands I commit my spirit!*" (Luke 23:34, 46).

Stephen's prayer reflects or images the prayer of Jesus.

Jesus himself teaches us how to pray: "When you pray, say: 'Father, hallowed be your name. Your kingdom come….'" (Luke 11:2). In the Lord's Prayer, also known as the "Our Father," Jesus invites us to pray to his Father, who answers the prayers of his children:

> ### Luke 11:9–10 (ESV)
>
> *And I tell you, ask, and it will be given to you; seek, and you will find; knock, and it will be opened to you. For everyone who asks receives, and the one who seeks finds, and to the one who knocks it will be opened.*

What we often miss about Luke's rendition of the Lord's Prayer is what—or more precisely, *whom*—we are supposed to be asking, seeking, and knocking for!

The answer: The Holy Spirit!

Jesus compares earthly fathers to his heavenly Father. If earthly fathers, who are not that great when compared to God the Father, give their children "good gifts" when they ask, *"how much more will the heavenly Father give the Holy Spirit to those who ask him!"* (11:13).

Jesus teaches us to ask the Father for the gift of the Spirit!

In his Small Catechism, Martin Luther picked up on this truth in his explanation of the second petition of the Lord's Prayer. When we pray, *Thy kingdom come*, how exactly does God answer this prayer?

Luther responds that God's kingdom comes to us "whenever our heavenly Father gives us his Holy Spirit, so that through his grace we believe his Holy Word and live godly lives here in time and hereafter in eternity" (The Lord's Prayer, The Second Petition, KW 8).

God's kingdom comes when we pray for the gift of the Spirit!

God's kingdom or ruling in our midst happens in our lives when we ask his Holy Spirit to lead us to believe his Word and live holy lives. Here faith and life go together: To live godly lives is to live by faith in Christ.

This is all the work of the Holy Spirit for us and in us. As Luther puts it, to confess *"I believe in the Holy Spirit,"* means that "I cannot believe in Jesus Christ my Lord or come to him, but instead the Holy Spirit has called me through the gospel, enlightened me with his gifts, made me holy and kept me in the true faith..." (The Creed, The Third Article, KW 6).

Knowing that our Father has promised to give all good gifts to his children, let us gladly take to heart Jesus' invitation and ask God to send us his Holy Spirit each and every day! *Come, Holy Spirit!*

The songs of the Church contain a long tradition of prayers to and for the Holy Spirit. One famous medieval hymn comes to mind: *Veni Creator Spiritus* (Come, Creator Spirit).

The first stanza in *The Lutheran Service* Book reads:

> *Come, Holy Ghost, Creator blest,*
> *And make our hearts Your place of rest;*
> *Come with Your grace and heav'nly aid,*
> *And fill the hearts which You have made.*

The same Spirit who created and sustains the big wide world also comes to dwell in our little hearts, to fill with his grace what he has made!

Yet we must not think of the Spirit as our possession, but rather as *"the Lord and Giver of life"* (Nicene Creed). The Holy Spirit is God; we are not. Yes, the Spirit of God freely and graciously dwells, rests in us. Yet we call upon the Spirit at all times on account of our need. We always need the Spirit to work in and through us.

Another special medieval hymn is *Veni Sancte Spiritus* (Come, Holy Spirit). One of the stanzas reads:

> *Cleanse that which is unclean,*
> *Water that which is dry,*
> *Heal that which is wounded.*

These are images of renewal, of the Spirit as the water of life. They remind us to call upon the Spirit to cleanse us from sin, refresh us with his presence in our spiritual thirst, and heal our broken hearts. Then there is this stanza:

> *Bend that which is inflexible,*
> *Fire that which is chilled,*
> *Correct what goes astray.*

Here the Spirit is pictured as a burning fire that bends, warms up, and straightens. We can easily think of a sculptor who molds and shapes metal with the fire of his love.

And then, there is Luther's "Come, Holy Ghost, God and Lord." The third stanza (LSB 497) follows up on the language of the Spirit as a fire that molds:

> *Come, holy Fire, comfort true,*
> *Grant us the will Your work to do*
> *And in Your service to abide;*
> *Let trials turn us not aside.*
> *Lord, by Your pow'r prepare each heart,*
> *And to our weakness strength impart*
> *That bravely here we may contend,*
> *Through life and death to You, our Lord, ascend.*
> *Alleluia, alleluia!*

The Spirit is the fire from above that makes us holy, granting us the will to work and serve, shaping us to be a sacrifice pleasing to the Lord.

The Spirit makes us brave by giving us his power and strength to stand firm through the trials of life, so that we might be faithful to God in life and death.

When we sing, "*Come, Holy Ghost,*" we are calling upon the same Spirit who sustained Stephen in his trials as he served God, even unto death.

Seeing how Jesus, Luther, and the Church's song throughout time all teach us to pray for the gift of the Holy

Spirit, who comes from the Father, we boldly and joyfully claim this gift in our lives today. *Come, Holy Spirit!*

Finally, let us remember that when we pray, *Come, Holy Spirit*, we are also asking the Sculptor Spirit to shape or conform us to be like Jesus.

Paul says that "*those God foreknew he also predestined to be conformed to the image of his Son*" (Romans 8:29). At Creation, the first humans were shaped "*in the image of God*" (Genesis 1:27). That image, though defaced by sin, was restored in Jesus, the New Adam, who is also "*the image of the invisible God*" (Colossians 1:15).

Since the Spirit joins us to Jesus in baptism, we also begin to be restored to the image of God in Jesus: "*Just as we have borne the image of the man of dust, we shall also bear the image of the man of heaven*" (1 Corinthians 15:49).

Of course, the final restoration of that divine image awaits the resurrection of the dead and the life of the world to come. But already now, ahead of time, the Spirit who raised Jesus from the dead is shaping that resurrection, New Creation life in us.

We are already now "*being transformed into his image with ever-increasing glory, which comes from the Lord, who is the Spirit*" (2 Corinthians 3:18).

This is the sanctifying work of the Spirit among us. The image of God, which was given at Creation and restored in Jesus, will again be fully ours in the New Creation. By the power of the Spirit, that New Creation life begins already now. And when the Spirit shapes New Creation life in us, the Spirit is conforming us to the image of Christ, making us look more and more like Jesus.

By leading us to die to sin and raising us to new life, the Spirit forms us to be like Jesus in a death and resurrection like his.

By sustaining us in the trials of life, the Spirit conforms us to be like Jesus, who was led by the Spirit into the desert to stand firm against the attacks of the evil one.

By giving us the will to serve others in God's name, the Spirit conforms us to be like Jesus, who came not to be served but to serve and to give his life as a ransom for many.

We speak of Christlikeness, not Christ-sameness. We are not the same as Christ. There is only one Jesus. But by God's grace, Jesus has sent the same Spirit who rests on him to rest and dwell in us, his disciples. And that Spirit continually molds us to be like Jesus as we grow in him through the Word.

To guide and equip you in the lifelong journey of Christlike discipleship, I commend the work of my friend and colleague Justin Rossow. Through his rich and insightful devotional writing, he will strengthen your knowledge of and trust in the Sculptor Spirit's formative work in your life.

As you begin this journey, let us pray:

> Come, Holy Spirit, and do your sculpting
> work in our hearts, minds, and lives. Shape
> and mold us to be like Jesus. Amen.

Leopoldo A. Sánchez M., PhD
Professor of Systematic Theology
Concordia Seminary
St. Louis, Missouri

Getting Ready

On the Road Again

Easter evening, as the day was coming to a close, two sorrowful and bewildered followers of Jesus found themselves on the road home. It wasn't a long trip, only about seven miles, but they walked with heavy hearts and a heavy step.

A man they didn't recognize suddenly shows up and walks with them on that lonely road. As they begin to talk, it's obvious the stranger has no concept of the current events causing such a stir. They have to tell this guy all about Jesus, the great prophet, and their hopes that he was the one to save Israel, and the devastating dashing of those hopes when their own religious leaders managed to get a Roman death sentence handed down.

They even mention their friends who made a confusing claim that very morning: they said Jesus' body was missing and angels were seen at the tomb.

That's when this stranger calls them foolish—not because of the fanciful claims of heavenly messengers and missing corpses—but because they are so slow to believe it.

What follows is a micro-small group Bible study of three that I would give anything to be a part of. (I imagine, in eternity, we each get to pick a friend and walk with Jesus for seven miles while he opens the Scriptures for us. It might not happen that way; but I call dibs, just in case.)

You know the story. The stranger walking with them in their grief and confusion and misunderstanding and slow faith was none other than the resurrected Jesus himself. Jesus walks them through the Old Testament and shows them the necessity of his own suffering and death and rising to life: as the Christ, the Anointed One, these were the things he *had* to do.

Of course, the Emmaus Road disciples (for that is where they were headed: the town of Emmaus) don't recognize the risen Christ until Jesus breaks the bread and gives it to them (wink, wink; nudge, nudge).

Then Jesus suddenly disappears, and the Emmaus Road rings with the clatter of sandals once again—no longer a heavy death knell of plodding footsteps, but the rapid staccato of beautiful feet that bring good news: Jesus is alive!

No sooner have these two finished telling their story to a group of uncertain disciples crowded into a locked room than Jesus himself shows up among them. The one who was present in their conversation on the road makes himself present as they share his story with others.

Jesus is met with skeptical joy. He even eats some leftovers so the disciples can see he has a real, physical body that can digest food and doesn't float across the floor.

Before the risen Lord is off again (you can't seem to keep Jesus in one place very long after the resurrection), Jesus commissions them as his witnesses and sends them out, even as Jesus was commissioned and sent by the Father.

In Luke's account, Jesus promises to send the Spirit, and commands these followers to wait in Jerusalem until they have been clothed with power, the kind of power that only comes from above.

The way John paints the picture, Jesus breathes on that mixed-up, disbelieving, troubled group of followers right then and there and says, "Receive the Holy Spirit."

Of course, John doesn't record the Day of Pentecost in his Gospel, and Luke still has Luke, Part II coming out. (The famous sequel to the Gospel of Luke is commonly known as the book of Acts.) Acts starts with the Ascension in Chapter 1 and the coming of the Spirit at Pentecost in Chapter 2.

These two very different authors often record very different parts of the story of Jesus (which helps give us a bigger picture). But as different as they are in focus, Luke and John are intimately linked in purpose as well as in detail.

In John, Jesus *breathes* on his disciples as he pours out the Spirit. That exhaling not only calls to mind God breathing life into humanity at creation, but the word for "breath" in Hebrew as well as Greek is the same word as "wind" and "spirit." So Jesus exhales the Holy Breath, or breathes out the Holy Wind, or spirits the Holy Spirit into his disciples.

In *Luke: The Sequel* (Acts 2), Peter says Jesus himself has poured out the Spirit. As you recall, that pouring came with a mighty *wind* (or mighty *breath*; or mighty *Spirit*) that shook the whole house. Both Luke and John are clear: Jesus pours out the Holy Spirit on his followers.

But check all of the Gospels and you'll find that Jesus is only completing an action that began at the very beginning of his ministry. The Jesus who *pours out* the Spirit is the same Jesus who first *received* the Spirit. In fact, to be the Christ, or Messiah, or "Anointed One" is to be the one anointed with the Holy Spirit, who receives, and bears, and ultimately pours out the Spirit on others.

Jesus is conceived by the power of the Holy Spirit (Luke 1:35). Jesus receives the Spirit in bodily form at his baptism (Matthew 3, Mark 1, Luke 3). With toes still dripping wet from the Jordan River, Jesus is led (or even "driven"!) into the wilderness by the Spirit to face the Tempter (Matthew 4, Mark 1, Luke 4). Jesus returns from the wilderness temptation in the power of the Spirit (Luke 4:14) and preaches and teaches as the Anointed-with-the-Spirit-One (Luke 4:16–21). Jesus is filled with joy in the Holy Spirit (Luke 10:21), promises the Holy Spirit (John 14:16–17), and from the cross (John 19:30), in the Upper Room (John 20), and on the Day of Pentecost (Acts 2) gives, breathes, and pours out the Spirit.

Given the defining role the Spirit plays in the ministry of the Messiah, who by definition is anointed with the Spirit, we should read Jesus' commission in John 20 like this:

"As the Father sent me *and gave me the Spirit to guide and empower the Father's mission through me*, so I am sending you: receive the Holy Spirit *to guide and empower my mission through you*."

The same Spirit who indwelt Jesus as the Christ dwells in you; the same Spirit who was poured out on Jesus at his baptism is poured out on you at yours. The same wind-breath-spirit that shook the house on Pentecost still blows where the Spirit wills; still fills and empowers and comforts and sends. The same Spirit who filled Jesus with joy fills your perpetual adventure of discipleship with holy curiosity and divine delight.

Jesus receives the Spirit, for you. Jesus bears the Spirit, for you. Jesus pours out the Spirit on you. And, just as the ministry of Jesus *for you* is tied to the work of the Spirit, so the work of the Spirit *in you* is tied to ministry of Jesus. You can't separate the two. What Jesus did *for you*, the Spirit shapes *in you*. That's what this faith journey is all about.

As you walk your own Emmaus Road, somewhat lost and burdened, you find a Traveling Companion who wants to know all about your dashed hopes and confused faith. You have Someone who walks with you, and opens Scripture, and sets your heart aflame. You recognize that Someone in the breaking of the bread. And, as you tell your story, that same Someone shows up to give you his own peace and to breathe out the Spirit once again.

The Work of the Sculptor Spirit

In his book *Sculptor Spirit: Models of Sanctification from Spirit Christology*, Leopoldo A. Sánchez M. goes into detail about the ways the Scriptures and the Early Church portray the work of the Spirit as shaping the life and ministry of Jesus in us.

The five key models from Leo's book (slightly modified) help provide a map and a trailhead for our journey over the next six weeks. As we look at how the Holy Spirit conforms our lives to the same life the Spirit shaped and empowered in Jesus, we will explore these five ways of viewing the work of the Spirit in us:

(1) Renewal: Daily dying and rising in baptism.
The Spirit who raised Jesus from the dead shapes Jesus' death and resurrection in us. We daily walk in the waters of our own baptism, drowning our old, sinful, selfish nature and rising daily to new life.

(2) Spiritual Warfare: Struggle and temptation.
Jesus faced the tempter in the desert and in the Garden; the Spirit shapes in us Jesus' dependence on God's Word in the face of trial and temptation.

(3) Pouring: Filled up and overflowing to others.
Just as Jesus received the Spirit and then poured himself out in service for others, so we receive the Spirit from Jesus and overflow into the lives of the people around us.

(4) Hospitality: A heart for outsiders.
The Spirit led Jesus to encounter people on the margins; the Spirit shapes in us Jesus' heart of welcome for the marginal and marginalized.

(5) Rhythm: A pattern of rest, work, and play.
Just as Jesus knew work, rest, and refreshment in the Spirit, so we find a Spirit-led rhythm of rest, work, and play.

In all of these ways, and more, the same Spirit who filled Jesus, and led Jesus, and empowered Jesus, and gave Jesus joy now fills, leads, empowers, and gladdens you on your journey of faith.

Your job in all of this is not to put Jesus up on a pedestal as the gold standard you are supposed to strive to reach. Rather, the Spirit brings Jesus near to you and shapes Jesus in you. You are actively engaged in this process; and at the same time, you are completely dependent on the Spirit, even when you are most active in your following.

So the pressure is off. When this book is done, you won't be graded on your holiness, or your effort, or your ability to pray, or even the consistency of your dependence on the Spirit.

Instead, God is already now rejoicing that you have put your foot on this path. Jesus has a twinkle in his eye as he looks ahead to your prayers and struggles and joys and questions. The Spirit who connects the Father and the Son now takes up residence in your heart, and makes the Father and the Son present to you, too.

This whole journey is a gift of grace. The Spirit will fill you and lead you and shape you and use you. Jesus will be present with you and for you. And the Father will rejoice over you with singing.

We pray, "Come, Holy Spirit." And we entrust our lives and eternities to the promised answer: *"How much more will your Father in heaven give the Holy Spirit to those who ask!"* (Luke 11:13, NIV).

Day 1, Saturday

Begin with Rest

Welcome to this journey of discipleship! The next weeks will bring you into the presence of Jesus and invoke the formative power of the Holy Spirit. You are embarking on an adventure of discovery in God's Word that promises to strengthen your faith and shape your life. You stand on the threshold of discovering treasures both new and old, so it's important that you make a good start.

Are you ready? OK! Time to take a break!

No, seriously. That's all for today. Get some rest. Take a nap if you are able. Take the time you have set aside to spend with God, and spend it with God in rest.

Don't get back to your weekend routine just yet. Linger a little longer. You aren't doing nothing; you are engaged in some very important Kingdom work, the work of dependence, of being still, of breathing in and breathing out and trusting God to take care of the rest.

Even Jesus could be found snatching a few z's, at times to the consternation of his followers. Being shaped to be like Jesus also means this: sometimes your *work* is *resting* in the Spirit.

So get to work, and don't do anything for seven whole minutes! (Set a timer if you have to...) If it helps you rest, write down whatever tries to grab your attention on a list to worry about later. Right now, don't worry about anything.

Deep breath. Relax. Jesus has you right where he wants you. Just lean back and be still in the presence of God.

Psalm 4:8 (NIV)

In peace I will lie down and sleep, for you alone, LORD, make me dwell in safety.

Psalm 127:2 (NIV)

[The LORD] grants rest to those he loves.

Prayer

Come, Holy Spirit, and give me rest.

Quiet my anxious heart and mind.

Still my body and my soul.

Breath of Life, breathe in me,
and give me your peace. Amen.

Day 2, Sunday

Conformed to Jesus' Death and Resurrection

Watch any sculptor and you will see that the artist doesn't carve or mold or chisel or shape randomly or haphazardly, but intentionally and according to a clear design. Even if you don't understand why the sculptor had to remove that piece of marble, you know that the skillful artist always shapes with purpose.

When the Spirit shapes your life and your faith, you can trust the skill, intention, and design of that divine artist. The Spirit doesn't shape randomly or haphazardly; you are being shaped with intention and according to design. As Dr. Leo Sánchez said in the Foreword, the Sculptor Spirit is conforming you more and more to the image of Christ.

At the Very Beginning, the Sculptor Spirit hovered over the waters of creation. As the very first human was formed from clay, the Spirit breathed life into the human's form.

When Jesus took on flesh to undo the damage wrought by those first humans, the Spirit again hovered over the creation, and the Virgin conceived. As Jesus entered the waters of baptism, the Spirit alighted on him. As Jesus lay lifeless in a tomb, the Spirit breathed life into a lifeless lump of clay again, and the New Creation walked out of the grave.

The old, fallen creation still clings to you and calls to you from your past: you still know sin, and brokenness, and shame. The New Creation beckons you from your future: already now you know forgiveness, and renewal, and joy.

Into that tension steps the divine Sculptor. The Spirit shapes you daily and intentionally toward the pattern and beauty of the sacrificial death and New Creation life of Jesus. Even when you can't see it, your life is a work of art.

John 20:19–22 (NIV)

On the evening of that first day of the week, when the disciples were together, with the doors locked for fear of the Jewish leaders, Jesus came and stood among them and said, "Peace be with you!"

After he said this, he showed them his hands and side. The disciples were overjoyed when they saw the Lord.

Again Jesus said, "Peace be with you! As the Father has sent me, I am sending you."

And with that he breathed on them and said, "Receive the Holy Spirit."

Prayer

Resurrected Lord, breathe on me again today! Just as you personally breathed the Spirit of life into the human being you shaped from the dust, give me your personal, life-giving Spirit in abundance.

As I breathe in, I am aware of your presence; as I breathe out, I give my burdens to you.

My body breathes constantly, in and out, in and out, even as I sleep. I need to breathe to live. In the same way, I need your life-giving Spirit, Jesus, to sustain me.

Be as close and as present today as my breathing, and increase my dependence on you. Amen.

Watching for the Word

Sunday is a day of worship and prayer. Use this space to record something you saw, heard, read, or prayed today. What's Jesus speaking into your life?

Faith Experiment: A Moment to Breathe

Take a few minutes to focus on your breathing. Inhale to a slow count of 8 (the number of the New Creation); exhale to a slow count of 7 (the number of completion). Become aware of your breathing—taking in the new; releasing the old—as you take slow, deep breaths.

Once you've established a rhythm, turn your counting into prayer. As you breathe in, ask the Spirit to provide all that you need to support your body and your life of faith; receive the new. As you breathe out, ask the Spirit to remove your burdens, worries, and sinful stress; release the old.

Breathe with an awareness of the Spirit, the Breath of God, present and active in your life. Repeat this breathing experiment over the next few days or weeks, as you are led.

Where Two or Three Are Gathered

Talk about one or more of the following with a friend or family member.

How did you celebrate Easter as a kid? Who was usually present? What kinds of traditions have you held onto as you get older?

Have you ever witnessed an immersion baptism? Who was baptized and why were you there? What do you know about your baptism day?

Have you ever been in a situation where you could have died? What happened? How did it turn out? What did you take away from that experience?

Day 3, Monday

DOWN to Death and UP to Life

Because of the natural patterns of physical life in a physical world, UP for us humans is active and awake and healthy, while DOWN tends to be passive, sleepy, or sick. The sun rises (UP) and you wake UP and get UP and even grow UP. The sun goes DOWN and you slow DOWN and power DOWN and pray: "Now I lay me DOWN to sleep…"

Both literally and metaphorically, death is DOWN and resurrection is UP; no surprise there. But one DOWN in the Early Church defies our expectation: in the Nicene Creed we confess Jesus, who "came DOWN from heaven."

In all the other creedal statements for a hundred years before and after, that phrase "came DOWN" *never* means Jesus went from the Good (UP) to be with us here in the Bad (DOWN). Instead, when God comes DOWN to be with us, it's a sign of the End Times, the beginning of a New Creation where God and humans again walk together face to face.

When Jesus came DOWN, that was the beginning of The End. When you go DOWN into the baptismal waters and are buried with Christ DOWN in his tomb, you are joined to the one who came DOWN to be with you. When you rise UP daily from those death waters, you not only go UP to life: you begin living out the New Creation now, ahead of time. Your ultimate salvation comes not when you go UP to heaven when you die, but when Jesus comes DOWN one last time to inaugurate the resurrection of the dead and the life of the world to come.

In the UPs and DOWNs of your discipleship walk, remember this: Since you have already been raised UP with Jesus, the New Creation has already begun in you. Your eyes now look UP to watch for Jesus coming DOWN to you again today.

Romans 6:4 (ESV)

We were buried therefore with him by baptism into death, in order that, just as Christ was raised from the dead by the glory of the Father, we too might walk in newness of life.

Romans 8:29 (NIV)

For those God foreknew he also predestined to be conformed to the image of his Son.

Prayer

Spirit of Creation and New Creation,
join me to the death of Jesus.

Bury me deep in the watery grave of my baptism; kill my selfishness and pride. Join me to the death of Jesus that the sins of my past may have no power over me.

Then bring the power of Easter to my present reality. Raise me to newness of life even now, ahead of my eternal resurrection. Let the life of Jesus define my identity.

Fill me, change me, guide me, and overflow through me, to the glory of the Father.

Amen.

Meditation Quotation

"Calling brokenness by name does not mean we are inviting shame or blame; we are looking closer at it to see Hope more clearly."

—Heidi Goehmann (*Finding Hope*)

Personal Reflection

The *perfectionist* doesn't want to go down into the waters of baptism; the *fatalist* doesn't want to come back out.

Which is more like you? Do you typically tend to avoid admitting your sins? Or are you more likely to dwell on your sins, and avoid living out your forgiven identity?

Why do you think that is? Record your reflection below.

Imagination Experiment

When the Church was just becoming an official institution, your baptism would have gone something like this:

On the evening before Easter, you are led to a room below your local church. (At this point, having a whole building set aside for Christian worship is still something new.)

In the stone floor you see an octagonal baptismal basin, about three feet deep. You learned that the eight sides signify the *eighth* day, when the seven-day cycle of the Old Creation is broken and a New Creation begins. Jesus rose on the eighth day, and your baptism will be an eighth day, resurrection, New Creation event.

Ephphatha, the word Jesus breathed out in Mark 8 to open ears and lips, is also spoken over you, so your lips can speak words of faith. You face West to renounce the devil, and East to pledge fealty to the Kingdom of God. A prayer invokes the Spirit to hover over these baptismal waters.

At this point, the men and women are divided and attended to separately by deacons and deaconesses. You see, you are going down into these waters as buck naked as the day you were born. You set aside your old clothes, your old identity, and step into those New Creation waters.

Perhaps you kneel in the water. The Triune Name of God is spoken over you. So much water is poured over your head that you can hardly breathe. Gasping for air, you come up out of the flood, receive an anointing of oil and the Spirit, and towel off in time to put on new clothes.

Healed and sealed, clean and redeemed, you head upstairs where the rest of the congregation welcomes you and a candlelight service is about to begin. As Easter morning dawns, you receive Communion for the first time.

Imagine experiencing that story. What stands out for you?

Day 4, Tuesday

Come, Creator Spirit

As a nation of shepherds and farmers, the ancient Israelites preferred solid ground beneath their feet. The dark, churning waters of a storm-tossed sea took root in the Hebrew imagination as a symbol for all things chaotic, unreliable, powerful, and scary. You can't trust the sea. The sea has no order. Chaos is a monster too powerful to control.

God's view of chaos (and of monsters) is very different. The LORD rules over chaos as well as order. God rides the tempest and frolics with sea monsters. The Spirit hovers playfully over primal chaos and delights in the variety of sea creatures as well as in the order of the land. Filled with the Spirit, Jesus walks the deep as calmly as the shore and calls the wind and waves to heel. Chaos, like order, serves and obeys its maker.

Maybe Chaos and Order aren't two opposing forces, like Good and Evil, but complementary tools in the hands of the Creator Spirit. Doesn't true creativity have an element of both chaos and order? If you've ever known a creative artist, you could probably tell by their work-space or studio that chaos plays an important role in the creative act. But ask any artist who produces regular, quality work and they will also talk about the need for structure and rhythm and schedule and order. Chaos and order both serve creativity.

The next time your life feels chaotic and scary and out of control, take a deep breath. Invoke the Spirit who hovers over chaos. Don't pray for the chaos to simply go away; instead, ask the Spirit of Creation and New Creation to harness order and chaos at the same time, and use those tools to make something beautiful and useful out of your life.

Come, Creator Spirit! Rule the chaos and the order of our lives, to your glory! Amen.

Genesis 1:2 (ESV)

*The earth was without form and void, and
darkness was over the face of the deep.*

*And the Spirit of God was hovering over the
face of the waters.*

Prayer

Come, Holy Spirit, creator of all things!
Take in hand the chaos of my hectic week
and order my days after the Father's will.

Hover over today's needs and desires;
be present in my thinking, feeling, and
speaking. Bring peace to my turmoil, trust
to my uncertainty, energy to my work, and
inspiration to my routine.

Use your creative power to harness both the
chaos and the order of my life. Then craft
the beautiful life of Jesus in me. Amen.

Hymn Verse Prayer

Veni, Creator Spiritus,
mentes tuorum visita,
imple superna gratia,
quae tu creasti, pectora.

Come, Holy Ghost, Creator blest,
And make our hearts Your place of rest;
Come with Your grace and heav'nly aid
And fill the hearts which You have made.

Before Christmas we sing to Jesus: "Veni, Emmanuel! O come, O come, Emmanuel." In a similar way, we also sing for the Spirit promised by Jesus: "Veni, Spiritus; Come!"

This ancient hymn has been shaping the prayers of God's people for over 1,200 years. You can find versions of it in many hymnals. The tune is also one of the most famous examples of Gregorian chant.

Try finding this song online and maybe even singing along until the tune gets stuck in your head; or write out the first verse on a notecard (in Latin and/or in English) and carry it with you in your pocket or phone case.

In what ways can you intentionally take the prayer, "Come, Creator Spirit!" into the chaos and routine of your week?

Day 5, Wednesday

Clothed in Joy

Your outfit can say a lot about who you are or your intentions for the day. You dress one way to go to the beach; another way to perform brain surgery. Your clothes can even be a clue to your country or family of origin.

I remember one Easter, not too long ago, when my young son and I dressed in matching outfits: the same fancy tie, the same dapper vest, the same dress slacks. My boy was so proud to look like his dad. I have to tell you, my heart was full of joy to stand next to him in those new clothes!

That joyful family resemblance is part of what the Spirit is up to in your life. Through faith, you have put off the dirty work clothes you wore to do the job of sin and death. You set aside an old way of life when you went down into the bathwater of baptism, and it just wouldn't be right to put the old, stinky clothes back on. Instead, the Spirit clothes you with a new, clean robe; a robe of righteousness that belongs to, and in a sense actually *is*, Christ.

Like the Prodigal Son in the story, you end up with borrowed party clothes. They don't fit you perfectly yet, but you will continue to grow into them. And wearing them makes a certain family resemblance clear: you proudly stand next to your Father and say, "Dad! Look at me! I'm starting to look like you!"

That moment of recognition is filled with joy. (These are party clothes, after all.) And the best part is, the joy you have in wearing your new, resurrection, Jesus-robes is matched by the joy of the Father, who welcomes you home and orders the party to begin!

Galatians 3:27 (NIV)

*All of you who were baptized into Christ
have clothed yourselves with Christ.*

Luke 15:21–24 (ESV)

*The son said to him, "Father, I have sinned
against heaven and before you. I am no longer
worthy to be called your son."*

*But the father said to his servants, "Bring
quickly the best robe, and put it on him, and put
a ring on his hand, and shoes on his feet. And
bring the fattened calf and kill it, and let us eat
and celebrate. For this my son was dead, and is
alive again; he was lost, and is found." And
they began to celebrate.*

Prayer

Come, Holy Spirit, sculptor from on high!
Chisel away the rough edges of my selfish
heart and mold me more and more into
the image of Christ.

Give me that image as my new garment;
clothe me with Jesus; cover me with his
Easter life, so that by faith in him I joyfully
put on his resurrection power.

A free and forgiven heir of the New Creation,
I want to walk in the steps of the risen Son
and live out my calling as an heir of promise.
Spirit, make me look like Jesus. Amen.

Faith Experiment: Key Concept Calendar

Looking back on this first week so far, what stands out to you most from the days you were able to read, pray, or do a Faith Experiment? What caught your attention or your imagination? What hit home? What did you circle, or highlight, or underline?

Could you summarize those key takeaways in a single word or short phrase? Could you sketch a simple object to capture the dynamic of an idea and make it memorable?

Beginning on page 140 in the back of this book, you will find a daily calendar for the first five weeks of this study where you can record the most important thing the Spirit is placing on your heart each day.

Take some time this week to record on that calendar your takeaway for each day you have done so far. Use a word, an image, or a short phrase. Whenever you sit with the readings and prayers from a specific day, reflect on what caught your attention most, and add something to your Key Concept Calendar at the back of the book.

Be forewarned: you will most likely have some blank days on your calendar. That's OK. You are only on day five, and maybe you have missed a day or two already. Just keep moving forward, one day at a time. Don't feel like you have catch up or get everything done. Allow the days you are able to engage to be their own blessing, without bearing the guilt of days you have missed.

By week six, you will be able to look back at a patchwork quilt of what Jesus has been speaking into your life by his Word and Spirit. However much or little you have filled in, the pattern will be a beautiful reminder of your time spent with God.

Day 6, Thursday

Purifying Fire

Under the right circumstances, fire provides protection and guidance. Fire cooks food and warms bodies. Fire can sterilize, or cauterize, or purify. Fire is also dangerous, so harnessing the destructive power of fire takes special care.

Take metallurgy as an example. Get gold or silver hot enough, and you can remove any foreign substance that dulls or weakens. But get that fire too hot and it will damage the metal itself. The difference between pure gold and a ruined lump of worthless metal can be mere moments over the flame. So the refining process takes years of experience to learn and the artist's full, focused attention to achieve.

The Holy Spirit is like that. While the fire of the presence of the Spirit in your life can inspire and warm and enlighten, the Spirit also burns, kills, consumes, and purifies.

When the precious metal of your faith is in the crucible, it's natural to feel threatened by the flames. You are in real danger, and the parts of you that belong to your old, sinful nature will be consumed by the process.

But this refining fire is not some random blaze. The Divine Craftsman has the skill, and patience, and experience to preserve the pure metal through the fire.

God's careful attention is focused on you most at the moment you are being refined.

When the Holy Spirit works in your life as a purifying fire, trust the heart of the Artist beyond the experience of the flames. Your faith is more precious to Jesus than silver or gold. Your faith and your future are in good hands.

Matthew 3:11 (ESV)

He will baptize you with the Holy Spirit and fire.

1 Peter 1:7 (NIV)

These [trials] have come so that the proven genuineness of your faith—of greater worth than gold, which perishes even though refined by fire—may result in praise, glory and honor when Jesus Christ is revealed.

Prayer

Come, Holy Spirit, fire from above! Burn away my sins and purify my heart with God's love, so that my life mirrors Christ's faithfulness and service.

O Holy Fire, you who kill and make alive, I confess my sins to you today. I hold nothing back, known or unknown. I especially need forgiveness for ...

Consume my dross with your flame; put to death everything in me that opposes your purpose; kindle in me a faith that trusts you.

Amen.

Meditation Quotation

The disciples at Pentecost "partook of fire, not of burning but of saving fire; of fire which consumes the thorns of sins, but gives lustre to the soul. This is now coming upon you also, and that to strip away and consume your sins which are like thorns, and to brighten yet more the precious possession of your souls, and to give you grace."

—Saint Cyril of Jerusalem
(c. 313–386 A.D.)

Personal Reflection

A purifying fire can do damage, but if controlled properly, it consumes only the imperfections that taint or stain. Have you had an experience of being refined through fire? What did you lose? What did you gain? How did you pray in the midst of the fire? Share your story with a friend.

Where do you think the Holy Spirit is killing or raising, refining or sculpting you right now?

Faith Experiment: Purifying Fire

Take time this week to write down the imperfections and impurities in your life or heart that burden you the most; then burn away that dross with purifying flame. Any kind of paper will do, and any kind of fire. (Just be careful! Harnessing the power of fire takes focused attention and care.) You may find it cathartic to commit your sins to the Spirit of Jesus as you commit the paper you wrote them on to the flames.

Day 7, Friday

One Body; One Spirit

Human beings are unique in all creation: God designed us to be physical *and* spiritual creatures. God gave us bodies and souls that belong together.

That's one reason why death is such an affront to God's glory and power and intention and design. You were not created to be a temporary, mortal body that momentarily houses an eternal soul; your immortal soul belongs in an immortal body. But what God designed to go together, sin now pulls asunder. Death is the final, physical consequence of brokenness between God and humans and between humans and God's perfect creation. And the Resurrection of the Dead is the final victory over that separation: God finally putting human bodies and souls back together the way they were designed in the first place.

The Bible can sometimes talk about the people of God collectively as a body or temple; but empty bodies and empty temples are no good for anything. A body needs a soul; a temple needs the very presence of God.

We are each individual stones in a massive edifice. We are being built together into a beautiful structure where heaven meets earth and the Spirit of God takes up residence.

We are each individual parts of a living, breathing, human body—the Body of Christ. Each of us has unique gifts and functions we bring to the whole as we, together, bring the life and activity of Jesus to the world. And the soul that enlivens the body is the same Spirit who fills the temple.

The Holy Spirit dwells in you as an individual; but the Spirit also resides in us, together, as the Body of Christ.

1 Corinthians 12:11–13 (NIV)

All these are the work of one and the same Spirit, and he distributes them to each one, just as he determines. Just as a body, though one, has many parts, but all its many parts form one body, so it is with Christ. For we were all baptized by one Spirit so as to form one body— whether Jews or Gentiles, slave or free—and we were all given the one Spirit to drink.

Ephesians 2:21–22 (ESV)

In him the whole building is joined together and rises to become a holy temple in the Lord. And in him you too are being built together to become a dwelling in which God lives by his Spirit.

Prayer

Lord God, Heavenly Father, thank you for arranging the members of the Body so carefully! Thank you for the variety of your gifts, and for the unique life you continue to give me to use for your glory.

Thank you for my friends and the gifts I see them using, especially ...

Give us to drink again of the one Spirit that binds your people together. Give your Church one heart and one mind, that we may speak with one voice. Bring unity in our division, Lord, and give us your Spirit of Peace, for the sake of Jesus. Amen.

Day 8, Saturday

The Rest of a Child

No one sleeps quite as soundly as a child. You've seen it before, right? The toddler, playing hard all day, is now up past her bedtime. Depending on the child's age and on the situation, being over-tired can bring other complications; but for now, remember a time when that little kid finally wore out, found mom or dad, and crashed.

You know the scene: the little head bobs from side to side for a moment. The pudgy cheeks are flushed like sunset. Eyes droop and flutter and then finally, blissfully, shut tight. The sleep that child enjoys is like no other: safe and warm, loved and held.

That's also an image of your relationship with your Heavenly Father. You are safe and warm, loved and held. Confidence in that relationship allowed Jesus to sleep soundly even on a boat in the midst of a storm. Confidence in that relationship invites you to set aside the concerns and complications that come from being over-busy and over-tired, and simply rest.

The Spirit puts the prayer of a trusting child on your lips: "*Abba*, Father." The Spirit shapes the trusting confidence of the Son in your heart. The Spirit invites you, after a hard week, to lay your head down on your Father's shoulder and soak up the sense that you are loved and held.

If you skipped any readings this week, you could go back and pick up what you missed. But you don't have to. Maybe the invitation today is just to be at peace; to not strive to catch up on anything at all; to rest in the confidence that the world is a big and scary place, but you are loved by the One who made the world. Good night. Sleep well. Your Father has the situation well in hand.

Romans 8:14–16 (NIV)

For those who are led by the Spirit of God are the children of God. The Spirit you received does not make you slaves, so that you live in fear again; rather, the Spirit you received brought about your adoption to sonship. And by him we cry, "Abba, Father."

The Spirit himself testifies with our spirit that we are God's children. Now if we are children, then we are heirs—heirs of God and co-heirs with Christ, if indeed we share in his sufferings in order that we may also share in his glory.

Prayer

Loving Father, thank you for Your Spirit, who lives in me. What an amazing thought! The same Spirit who raised Jesus from the dead also gives me life!

Come, Holy Spirit, Spirit of Adoption, and empower me to cry out, *"Abba,* Father!"

Fill me with the dependence that brings true peace. Help me trust that what is too big for me is not too big for my *Abba.*

Shape the confidence of Jesus in me, that I may rest secure, even when tossed about.

Come, Holy Spirit, and give me childlike faith, and childlike rest. Amen.

Day 9, Sunday

Wilderness and Garden

At the very, very beginning, God lovingly placed handcrafted human beings in the midst of a mountain paradise. That first garden/temple became a place of testing when the devil, that sneaky old snake, challenged the boundaries of obedience and promise.

As part of a rescue plan to heal the divide left by that first sin, God chose a people in grace and led them out of slavery to a mountain, and then, into a wilderness where they were also tested and tempted. These people of God failed, too.

Jesus, in his life and ministry, walks in the footsteps of God's people. Led into the wilderness by the Spirit in order to be tempted by the devil, Jesus clings to God's Word in ways God's people failed to do.

Jesus also finds himself in a garden, where he fervently prays for the Cup of Suffering to pass him by. But where the first humans sought a path apart from God's Word, this New Human clings to God's Word and climbs up the mountain of Golgotha to submit his future to God's plan.

Jesus walks into the wilderness and garden in your shoes and makes your temptation struggles his own. As the Spirit shapes the life of Jesus in you, you also walk into the wilderness and garden in *his* shoes: you step where Jesus stepped; you hold to the Word as Jesus held to the Word; you submit your life and future to God's good pleasure, even as Jesus did in the Garden of Gethsemane.

The old, sinful humanity still clings to you; but the first New Creation Human also claims you as his own. You are never alone in the wilderness and garden: you stand with Jesus, who stood with you.

Luke 4:1 (NIV)

*Jesus, full of the Holy Spirit, left the Jordan
and was led by the Spirit into the wilderness.*

Prayer

Holy Spirit, Faithful Companion of Pilgrims,
join me to Jesus on his journey into the
wilderness. Equip and prepare me to meet
the challenge of trial and temptation.

Holy Spirit, Creative Wind, make the garden
of my testing a time for me to grow in Word
and in prayer.

Holy Spirit, Rain from Heaven, do not let me
be tempted beyond what I can bear, but
refresh me and restore me.

Join me to Jesus and his triumph over the
Tempter, and lead me to the Paradise of
restored relationship with God. Amen.

Watching for the Word

Sunday is a day of worship and prayer. Use this space to record something you saw, heard, read, or prayed today. What's Jesus speaking into your life?

Day 10, Monday

This Means War

Filled with the Holy Spirt at his baptism, Jesus launches a major tactical offensive. His preaching and healing send a clear message: "The time is now. The Kingdom of God is at hand. Repent and believe the Good News."

It's no wonder the devil chooses this moment to mount a counterattack. The baptism of Jesus is a declaration of all-out war.

In fact, your baptism is, too. In your baptism, you renounce the devil and all his works and all his ways. From that day forward, you will be under attack by the one who hates to see sin forgiven, doubt healed, and relationships restored. Your baptism is a declaration of war.

The fact that you struggle with temptation in your life is actually a gracious gift (even if it doesn't feel like it). Think about it: if you didn't *struggle* with temptation, you would already belong completely to the enemy. Temptation is only combat for you because, as a citizen of a heavenly kingdom, you are at war with the kingdom of sin and death.

That declaration of war is as old as sin itself. Immediately after Adam and Eve chose the side of darkness over light, God says to the Serpent, "I am going to put enmity, *warfare*, between you and the woman; between your offspring and hers." The Almighty has to *create enmity* between them; at that point in the story, and by their own choice, *the humans and the devil are on the same side*.

So God declares war. God promises a Seed of the Woman able to crush the Serpent's head. God won't let you go without a fight. Like the baptism of Jesus, your baptism sends a clear message to the forces of death and hell.

This means war.

Genesis 3:15 (ESV)

I will put enmity between you and the woman,
  and between your offspring and her offspring;
he shall bruise your head,
  and you shall bruise his heel.

Romans 13:12 (NIV)

The night is nearly over; the day is almost here.
So let us put aside the deeds of darkness and put
on the armor of light.

Prayer

Come Holy Spirit, defender of the saints!
Make me vigilant and alert; let me not fall
into the devil's snares.

You know where I am weak and vulnerable.
You know my spiritual Achilles' heel. You
know the strength and wisdom I need from
you today.

As you led Jesus into the desert, so lead me
also in Jesus' name to pray and trust in
God's Word without fail.

Declare war again on the forces of darkness
in my heart and in my life. Be my courage
and my safety in the fray, and equip me
with the baptismal armor of light, that the
evil foe may have no power over me. Amen.

Meditation Quotation

"The Christian life does not make us immune
to the attacks of the devil, but the object of
those attacks."

—*Leopoldo A. Sánchez M. (Sculptor Spirit)*

Faith Experiment: Key Concept Calendar

Don't forget to add an image, word, or phrase to your Key
Concept Calendar at the back of this book as you go. You
can find more direction on page 28.

Personal Reflection

Do you know what your "spiritual Achilles' heel" is?

If you don't know, how you might you identify a recurring
weakness or point of attack?

If an area of vulnerability comes to mind, do you have a
trusted friend you could invite into your struggle so you
don't battle alone? We follow Jesus better when we follow
him together.

Faith Experiment: Remembering Your Baptism

I remember a woman in her eighties who was inspired to research her own baptism. She found the date, but the congregation where she was baptized had closed. She wanted a tangible reminder of that event, so she asked her church and we printed a new baptism certificate for her.

Do you know your baptism birthday? If you do, record it in the front of this book. Do you still have your baptism certificate? Then capture details like location, sponsors, pastor, etc. below the date. Those tangible reminders of God's promise to you can help you remember and rely on the Spirit poured out on you at your baptism.

If you don't have a baptismal certificate, do some family research and create your own. If you don't know when you were baptized, pick a date that is meaningful for you and celebrate your baptism on that day every year.

OR, for the adventurous of heart, research some historical declarations of war and then write one for your baptism.

Pro tip: a declaration of war typically (1) recognizes a situation that already exists, (2) lists major grievances against the enemy nation or kingdom, and (3) authorizes the use of all available resources to ensure victory.

How would you describe the current state of antagonism between the Kingdom of Darkness and the Kingdom of the Light? What are some of the grievances you would list against sin, death, and devil? What resources does the Kingdom of Heaven have at its disposal to carry out this war?

Your baptism certificate is a kind of declaration of war. Print out the document you created and keep a copy in this book to look back on when you feel especially weary or vulnerable or under attack. You are not in this alone.

Day 11, Tuesday

Go Pick a Fight

When I read Paul talking about putting on the "full armor of God," I used to think of a knight in medieval armor with a helmet, visor, metal gloves, chest plate, shining boots, and greaves. Then I realized how anachronistic a *medieval* suit of armor was, so now I just imagine Iron Man. (I mean, if you are going to be wrong anyway, you might as well be able to fly and shoot repulsor rays out of your palms, right?)

Whether you imagine wearing a full suit of armor like a knight, or stepping into the Iron Man armor, or something a little closer to the Roman outfit Paul had in mind, I think Paul's intention remains the same: Paul wants you to feel strong, and safe, and powerful, and ready for a fight.

I think sometimes the scandal of our Christian struggle with sin is that there isn't any. We know we remain sinners this side of eternity. We already know we will fail; and we know there will be forgiveness, so why bother? We never quite get around to the *warfare* part of spiritual warfare.

What if, this week, you chose to pick a fight? You decided to stand your ground? You refused to give in to the very first temptation that crossed your path?

What if it took *two* spiritual attacks before you let loose your tongue, or gave in to selfishness, or indulged your sinful pride? In the struggle against temptation, you will get battered and beaten. You will fall and fail. But do you sometimes give up and roll over before the struggle has even begun? That's not what Paul had in mind.

You are clothed with power from on high. You wear the Armor of Light. You are strong and safe and ready.

Go pick a fight.

Luke 24:49 (NIV)

I am going to send you what my Father has promised; but stay in the city until you have been clothed with power from on high.

Ephesians 6:17–18 (ESV)

Take the helmet of salvation, and the sword of the Spirit, which is the word of God, praying at all times in the Spirit.

Prayer

Come Holy Spirit, promise of the Father, and clothe me with power from on high!

Cover over my weakness with your strength. Wrap my frailty in your defenses. Arm me for the spiritual battle I will face today.

Since you declared war on the power of darkness in my life, be my light, my strength, and my shield. Conform me to the testing and the victory of my Lord Christ, in whose name I pray. Amen.

Day 12, Wednesday

Holding onto God's Delight

"Obedience to God's will" is a phrase we struggle to understand faithfully, but only because "obedience" and "God's will" don't actually mean what we think they mean. (I know! *Inconceivable*, right?)

God's "will" is what God desires, wants, or longs for because it brings such joy and delight. In fact, the word we typically translate "will" can sometime be translated "delight," and always has a shade of meaning related to joyful desire. God's *will* is also God's *delight*.

In contrast, when I hear people use the phrase, "God's will be done," they often seem to be talking about some cold, abstract design that, in the mysterious calculus of God's intentions, may bring about a good I never get to see.

But when Jesus teaches the disciples to pray, when Jesus himself prays, "Abba, Father, your will be done," Jesus isn't praying for a cold, calculating, abstract formula, but for the thing that will make the Father sing for joy.

Of course, as Jesus looks at the cross, it's difficult for him to see how that suffering could bring joy. But Jesus entrusts his death and his resurrection to the beautiful delight of the Father, confident not in the *math* behind the sacrifice, but in the *joy* that the Father sees clearly, but the Son is struggling to imagine.

So Jesus holds onto God's word of promise and takes a step forward in faith. That's actually what "obedience" is all about. Jesus isn't "following the rules." Jesus is holding on to God's promise for dear life. Jesus "obeys" God's "will." In other words, *Jesus holds onto God's delight for dear life.* By the power of the Spirit, so do you.

Hebrews 2:17–18 (NIV)

*For this reason he had to be made like them,
fully human in every way …*

*Because he himself suffered when he was tempted,
he is able to help those who are being tempted.*

Prayer

Come, Holy Spirit, anointing from above!
You empowered the Son's obedience to the
Father's mission, for me.

In the dangerous desert and garden, the
Son suffered the tempter's attacks; Jesus
knows deeply what I am going through.

I am tempted to be unfaithful. I struggle
with obedience. Spirit of God, let your
anointing help me discern what is right and
wrong, what is true and what is a lie.

In times of temptation, make me faithful
like Jesus to say: "Not my will, Father, but
yours be done." Shape in me the obedience
of the obedient Son. Teach me to hold on
for dear life to the Father's delight. Amen.

Day 13, Thursday

Sifted Like Wheat

Sifting seems like it wouldn't be fun for the wheat. The wheat gets tossed up in the air again and again and again. The chaff, part of the grain I'm sure the wheat still thinks it needs, gets blown on the wind and lost in the process. And then, just when the wheat has experienced peace and calm for a little while, it gets tossed up and turned around again! And again! And again! When you are being sifted, you are not in control.

But *someone* is in control. Someone is intentionally and repeatedly tossing that grain into the air to separate what is valuable from what will just blow away on the breeze.

Jesus tells Peter that Satan had to ask permission to sift the disciples like wheat. Satan isn't in charge. Satan isn't in control. Satan thinks this upheaval and turbulence will weaken and scatter the disciples. But God has an intention and a plan. God knows what will remain and what will be blown away. And God allows this sifting.

When your life feels out of control and your world is thrown up in the air, even when it's not your fault, even when it seems like there must be some malign will behind your turmoil, know that you will never be sifted except by God's permission and according to God's good purpose.

Before the sifting, Jesus says to Peter (using his pre-disciple name): "I have prayed for you, Simon, that your faith may not fail. When you have turned, strengthen your brothers."

As often as you have failed to pray that you would not fall into temptation, *Jesus has never failed to pray for you*. When your life is up in the air and out of control, when you are sifted, know that you are also covered by the prayers of Jesus.

Luke 22:31–32 (NIV)

"Simon, Simon, Satan has asked to sift all of you as wheat. But I have prayed for you, Simon, that your faith may not fail. And when you have turned back, strengthen your brothers."

Luke 22:40 (NIV)

On reaching the place, he said to them, "Pray that you will not fall into temptation."

Prayer

O, my Lord, my Teacher, my Friend—
how often I have failed you, Jesus!

How often I have failed to watch and pray!
How quickly I lose my focus, lose my
commitment, lose my way!

Do not treat me as my failures deserve.
Don't take your Holy Spirit from me, but
restore to me the joy of your salvation.

Strengthen my weak hands. Release me
from my past. Renew my prayers.

Let your Spirit intercede for me in my
weakness, and teach me to pray. Amen.

Personal Reflection

Think of a time when you felt far away from God. What kinds of things did other people do or say during that time? What things were not helpful? What helped most?

In the space below, write down something you would want someone to say to you when you feel sifted.

Prayer Experiment: The Secret Code Prayer

The Secret Code Prayer is a tool designed to help you focus and slow down when you pray. You can use this method to pray about anything. Today, take some time to talk to God about your prayer life.

What do you like about your pattern of prayer? What do you wish were different? What do you think the Spirit is shaping in you when it comes to prayer? Using a Secret Code Prayer for that conversation with God helps keep you focused, and also feels like your words are confidential.

Here's how this prayer experiment works:

1) Set a timer for five minutes.

2) Write out your prayer, one letter in each box of the graph card on the next page.

Choose all UPPERCASE or all lowercase letters, don't add spaces between words or punctuation, and don't worry about spelling. This is not a race; in five minutes, you might not fill in all the boxes, and that's OK.

3) When the timer goes off, finish your thought, add an Amen, and stop.

4) Reread what you wrote, slowly praying once more.

As you write one letter at a time in each box, you will tend to keep your word choices short and sweet, so your prayer may feel less formal and maybe even more intimate.

This practice is called a Secret Code Prayer because the end result looks like it needs to be decoded. Give it a try and see what you think!

Day 14, Friday

A Desert in Bloom

I remember visiting family in the arid wilderness region of Phoenix, Arizona, and the surrounding mountains. That landscape was so different from what I knew in Michigan growing up!

Of course, AZ is *hot;* but it's also *dry.* Almost everything has hard edges or pickers: rocks, insects, plants, and animals all seem sharp and pointy and dangerous. We didn't see many venomous snakes or ten-foot-tall cacti back home!

Though the greens are muted and a red/brown palette dominates the landscape, the desert has its own austere beauty. That is, until it rains.

I've only seen pictures, but I know that when it rains, the desert blooms. Bright yellows and purples cover the hills. Those giant saguaro cacti are crowned with tiny umbrellas of pink and white that they open against the rain. The land drinks in and is refreshed.

Wilderness wandering isn't only hard edges and venomous snakes. The Spirit can also lead to a hidden oasis, or cause rain to renew the hard-packed ground, or bring water from a rock. Although the arid wilderness is a place of testing and even temptation, God remembers it as a time when these beloved wanderers were daily dependent on the divine gift of daily bread. God even calls it a time of gentle courtship, when the Almighty tenderly sought a deepening relationship with a chosen people.

When you are in the arid wilderness of testing and temptation, there will be hard edges and spiky plants. But keep your heart and your eyes open: you will also know the refreshing renewal of a desert in bloom.

Isaiah 44:3 (ESV)

For I will pour water on the thirsty land,
and streams on the dry ground;
I will pour my Spirit on your offspring,
and my blessing on your descendants.

Prayer

Praise be to you, O Lord of heaven and earth! You pour out your Spirit on the tired and thirsty! You cause the desert to bloom with life! You give your gifts to generations of those who love you!

I thank you, Lord, for the gift of family and friends. Please rain down your Holy Spirit onto the lives of the people I love.

Today, I especially pray for ...

Give your Spirit freely, Lord, and refresh your people! Amen.

Where Two or Three Are Gathered
Talk about one or more of the following with a friend or family member.

Have you ever spent any time in an arid wilderness? Where? What was it like?

What's the most dangerous thing you have ever done? Did you feel safe? Why or why not?

If you knew you were going to end up stranded in the middle of the Arizona wilderness, who would you want with you, and why?

Day 15, Saturday

A Safe Place to Rest

Even in war, you don't spend every moment on the front lines. Of course, the enemy's attack could be unexpected, so a safe place to rest is vital for any army.

The imagery the Bible uses for spiritual warfare certainly includes the language of conflict and engagement and attack. But perhaps even more prevalent is the language of safety and protection and defense.

God's name is a strong tower you can run to in times of distress. God is a rock that provides shelter and stability. The presence of the Living God is a fortress and refuge, a shield, a hiding place, a stronghold and citadel.

In the dangerous adventure of following Jesus, you will get tired and worn out. Spiritual attack will beat you down. Always striving and struggling will leave you exhausted.

Take heart! The adventure of following Jesus isn't only striving and struggling! Jesus also invites his followers to find a quiet place with him and get some rest. Jesus welcomes the burdened and heavy-laden. Jesus both sends you out and gathers you in; empowers your battle and provides a safe place to rest.

Sometimes you have to stand and fight. When you do, you fight with the power of the Spirit of Jesus.

And sometimes you need to run and hide. When you do, you are surrounded and protected and shielded and renewed by the power of the Spirit of Jesus.

In your struggle and in your refuge, you belong to Jesus.

Psalm 91:2 (ESV)

I will say to the Lord,
"My refuge and my fortress,
my God, in whom I trust."

Prayer

Lord, you are my refuge and my fortress! Cover me with your presence and let me hide, safe and secure, under your wings. Let your faithfulness be my shield and sure defense.

I look around and see enemies, within and without, who are too strong for me. I grow weary of the hatred and animosity in the news. I am tired of the sinful leanings of my own heart. I feel worn down and exhausted.

Holy Spirit, I need a safe place to rest, a refuge from my struggle. Surround me with your presence and protect me when I am most vulnerable. Amen.

Day 16, Sunday

Filled up and Overflowing

How can you possibly be expected to pour into others if you aren't sure you are going to have enough yourself?

That fear of running out, of not having enough, of being empty seems to be a common theme in our culture. Consumerism is based on the basic principle that the consumer will never have enough. A quick internet search reveals our personal debt is almost three times our personal annual income. We need more, and need to spend more, even if we don't have it.

COVID hasn't slowed down our need. If anything, a pandemic heightens our sense of not having enough: not enough money, not enough time, not enough vaccinations or bandwidth or personal contact; not enough anything!

Jesus does call you to pour yourself out for other people; but Jesus does not intend for you to live your life on empty.

How is that possible?

Imagine you have a cup full of water and you are supposed to share that water with all the people in your life: your kids, your spouse, your coworkers, your neighbors, your parents, your friends … exhausting! And even if you run back to the kitchen sink to fill up, you spend half or more of your time with an empty cup. That's no way to live!

Now imagine you are one glass in a champagne fountain. You are constantly and perpetually pouring into the glasses around you because you are filled so much you overflow. That's the kind of life Jesus invites you into!

Jesus calls you to pour yourself out for other people because Jesus intends to fill you to overflowing.

Joel 2:28–29 (NIV)

I will pour out my Spirit on all people…
Even on my servants, both men and women,
I will pour out my Spirit in those days.

Prayer

Come, Holy Spirit, fill all the empty places of my life. Pour the power of your presence into my mind, my heart, and my attitudes.

Conform my way of seeing others to the way Jesus sees me, as he pours himself out to fill me up.

Spirit of abundance, don't hold back any gift or blessing I need in order to be a blessing to others. Whenever I feel dry or empty, gently turn me back to the cataract of your grace.

Let my cup overflow into the lives of others as I seek to live out the generous, out-pouring love of my Savior.

Teach me to give myself away, even as you give yourself to me without reservation.

Come, Holy Spirit, and fill me to overflowing. Amen.

Watching for the Word

Sunday is a day of worship and prayer. Use this space to record something you saw, heard, read, prayed, or sang today. What's Jesus speaking into your life?

Meditation Quotation

"Never-ending, unrelenting,
constant source of hope;
running down from lofty mountains
into springs below:

Oh, I am soaked from head to toe in
Grace, sweet grace; a fountain for my soul.
Grace, sweet grace; a mighty waterfall.

Drops of mercy all around;
everywhere the sound of Grace."

—Kip Fox, "The Sound of Grace"

Sketch Your Faith

Think of a situation in your life that involved LOTS of water.
Do a rough sketch of the scene, below.

Day 17, Monday

Upside-Down Authority

It's almost predictable, and kind of perplexing: time and time again, Jesus' closest friends hear him talk about his coming suffering, death, and resurrection and respond by arguing about which of them is the greatest. Why?

The disciples clearly don't have a clue that Jesus is going to *actually* die, let alone *actually* rise again. For the disciples, literal suffering and death seem out of the question for Jesus, precisely because he is the Christ, the Son of the Living God.

They see Jesus as a Power Messiah, come to restore God's Kingdom on earth and wielding all the authority of the Almighty. Maybe that's why Jesus talking about *dying* consistently brings up the topic of *power and authority*.

It all seems so typical—Jesus points to the cross, and his followers want to know who gets the gold star!

In one sense, the disciples are correct: Jesus the Messiah does wield the power and authority of the Kingdom. Jesus does establish God's eternal reign on earth (and, indeed, will come again in glory and power and authority to once and for all establish God's Kingdom, on earth as in heaven).

But in this time before the Very End of the story, Jesus exercises his power and authority to give himself away; to pour himself out; to suffer, and die, and rise.

That's the secret the disciples don't yet understand: heavenly authority makes the first last and the last first. Resurrection power lies down in the dust, to raise people of dust to New Creation life. And Jesus gives that upside-down power and authority to all who follow him.

Mark 10:45 (NIV)

For even the Son of Man did not come to be served, but to serve, and to give his life as a ransom for many.

Philippians 2:6–7 (ESV)

Though he was in the form of God, [Jesus] did not count equality with God a thing to be grasped, but emptied himself, by taking the form of a servant, being born in the likeness of men. And being found in human form, he humbled himself by becoming obedient to the point of death, even death on a cross.

Prayer

Jesus, you turn my world upside down! I think I know what authority looks like when I see business leaders or government officials; and then you come and show me what true power is.

You, who are equal with God, expressed your divine power by giving yourself away. You emptied yourself, poured yourself out, became a servant—became *my* servant.

Give me the faith to receive with open hands what you pour out. Then give me an attitude like yours to exert the authority of your Kingdom by giving myself away. Amen.

Day 18, Tuesday

Like Vine, Like Branches

At the beginning of his ministry, Jesus calls the ones he wanted for a dual purpose: (1) so they could be with him, and (2) so Jesus could send them out.

Jesus loved these disciples to the very end. Jesus himself washes their feet like a servant, then invites—commands, even!—that they also serve each other, and so find the completion not only of Jesus' love, but of his joy. Jesus (1) serves them, and then (2) releases them to serve.

That pattern of being called to be with Jesus first, and then to be sent out—to be served by Jesus, and then to serve—is summed up in the image of the vine and branches. Just after the foot washing, Jesus invites his disciples (you and me) into the mystery of the Trinity.

As the Spirit makes the Father abide with the Son, Jesus says, the Spirit will also make the Son abide with you. Jesus is (1) with the Father and (2) sent out by the Father in the Spirit. Jesus is the Vine, planted and nurtured and watered and pruned by the Father; the Vine who then gives life and nurtures and feeds the branches, who then bear fruit.

The branches belong to the Vine. As a branch, you are (1) connected to Jesus in the Spirit, and (2) sent out by Jesus in the power of the Spirit. You are *served*, and then you *serve*. You *receive life*, and then you *bear fruit*. You are called to be *with Jesus*, and called to be *sent out by Jesus*.

The Spirit who enables the Father to abide with Jesus also enables Jesus to abide with you. You are never called to serve or bear fruit on your own. You are chosen in delight to be *with Jesus*; and then, to be *like Jesus* in dependence and in service: like Vine, like branches.

Mark 3:13–14 (NIV)

Jesus went up on a mountainside and called to him those he wanted, and they came to him. He appointed twelve that they might be with him and that he might send them out

John 15:4 (ESV)

Abide in me, and I in you. As the branch cannot bear fruit by itself, unless it abides in the vine, neither can you, unless you abide in me.

Prayer

O Holy Spirit, you filled the Son of God with gifts to be our suffering Servant. Fill us also with your gifts, so that we may mirror our Lord's service to others.

Generous Spirit, graft me into the living Vine, the Lord Jesus Christ, that I may bear abundant fruit in my life.

Kill the weeds of my selfish pride that threaten to suffocate and hinder my growth. Fill me with Christ's patient love and teach me to share it with all. Amen.

Faith Experiment: Key Concept Calendar

Keep capturing your key takeaways on the calendar in the back of this book. When you're done, you'll have a way of looking back at all the different ways Jesus was active in your life. You can find the original description of this Faith Experiment on page 28. It's never too late to start!

Where Two or Three Are Gathered

Share a conversation with a friend or family member. Take some notes below.

Talk about three things you each see Jesus pouring into your life right now. Then talk about three things you each could pour into other people this week.

How does what you have to pour out relate to what Jesus has poured into you?

Day 19, Wednesday

Opening Your Clenched Fist

A clenched fist is an open hand turned in on itself. A fist doesn't need to grasp anything to be closed off to the rest of the world. A fist can be used as a weapon; but a fist can't offer or receive. A fist holds tightly and won't let go.

That may be why we fallen humans, turned in on ourselves, find it so difficult to forgive. Forgiving is a kind of letting go, releasing a burden, erasing a debt. Forgiving requires an open hand: you can't forgive with a closed fist.

Jesus knows how vulnerable forgiveness can make you. Jesus opened his hand to forgive, and we nailed it to a cross. Jesus extends an offer of grace that we can't receive as we stand with closed fists.

"She started it." "He did it on purpose!" "They'll do it again." Every sin against me is an affront to my autonomy, an offense against my pride. And my pride, turned in on itself, closes a fist on those sins and won't let go.

We have no easy answers or quick fixes for being turned in on ourselves. But Jesus teaches us to pray, "Forgive us our debts, as we forgive our debtors." It's not a matter of quid pro quo; it's a matter of physics. You simply cannot receive a free gift as long as your open hand is balled into a fist.

Opening that fist comes at great cost to your fallen, sinful nature: being crucified with Christ, putting your sinful self to death, so that the circle turned in on itself is broken. But opening that fist also comes with great gain: being raised with Jesus to new, resurrection life, even ahead of the resurrection. As a New Creation Human, you are turned outward to give and receive refreshing forgiveness freely, with your own open, nail-scarred and resurrected hands.

Matthew 6:12 (ESV)

*Forgive us our debts, as we also
have forgiven our debtors.*

Galatians 2:20 (NIV)

*I have been crucified with Christ and I no
longer live, but Christ lives in me. The life I
now live in the body, I live by faith in the Son of
God, who loved me and gave himself for me.*

Prayer

O Lord, I stand in your presence with closed
fists. I know I am holding onto my own guilt
and shame. I know I cling relentlessly to sins
committed against me.

Some people in my life do not deserve
forgiveness; and honestly, Lord, I don't even
want to forgive them.

Come, Holy Spirit, and soften my heart.
Gently open my hands to release the anger
and the hurt caused by other people. Give
me a willingness to forgive. Release me
from the weight of my own sin.

I open my hands in your presence, Lord.
I commit my debt and my debtors to your
care. Amen.

Personal Reflection

Record an experience of abundance. When have you had more than enough, more than you could use, so much you just had to share it with others?

What happened next?

Time, forgiveness, and money are all things we can be stingy with. What things to you tend to hold in a closed fist? What does it take to open your hand to receive what Jesus wants to give?

Mediation Quotation

"Our nature [is] so deeply *curved in on itself*
that it ... viciously seeks all things, even God,
for its own sake."

—Martin Luther (*Lectures on Romans*)

Prayer Experiment: Opening Your Clenched Fist

Take a few moments to use your body to help you pray. Begin by reflecting on some of the things you tend to hold tightly, like finances or time—things you find easy to horde and difficult to share. Or maybe you are holding onto hurt or resentment over what other people have done to you. Maybe you carry a burden of anxiety or shame or grief that you have tried to let go, but just can't.

Once you have something in mind, pray: "Come, Holy Spirit." Then clench your fist and hold it tight. Imagine you are clinging to that hurt or burden you don't want to let go. Keep holding it! Experience the tightness in your hand as your nails start to dig into your palm. Tighter! Feel your hand start to cramp or even shake. Hold it as long as you can, until you actually want to open that fist.

Holding onto that hurt or burden is no good for you, and no good for anyone else. Again pray: "Come, Holy Spirit!" and open your hand. Turn your open hand toward heaven and invite the Spirit to pour out just what you need to receive. If you have let go of resentment or someone else's sin, ask for refreshing forgiveness. If you have laid down grief or shame, ask for a renewal of your joy. Take a moment to receive with your open hand the good gifts the Spirit wants to give. When you find you have closed your fist around that burden once more, simply open your hand and pray again, as often as it takes, "Come, Holy Spirit!"

Day 20, Thursday

Filled With Joy

In cultures and languages around the world, we think about and experience our emotions as a kind of fluid in a vessel or container. Your heart, like a container, can feel empty or can overflow. Anger is often imagined as heated liquid under pressure: that's why people who are angry can "have steam coming out of their ears" or "blow their top."

Joy is another emotion that can fill the container of the heart with bubbling liquid, but joy is effervescent rather than heated to the boiling point. Joy isn't hot, though it can bubble up and even run over. When you experience joy, you might laugh, or shout, or jump up and spin around. You might even weep for joy: all that agitated liquid has to come out somehow! Joy can fill you to overflowing.

The emotions we experience as boiling liquids, like anger or even passion, can cool off quickly; you can throw a wet blanket on the fire, and when the temperature drops, the liquid emotion also settles down.

But you can't turn down or dilute joy quite as easily. Jesus shares his joy with his disciples right before being arrested, beaten, and condemned to die. None of that can steal Jesus's joy.

Even after Jesus ascended to heaven, the defining experience of those who came to know and follow him, sometimes in the face of opposition and persecution, was the experience of being filled with joy.

Look for ways the Spirit is filling you with resilient and effervescent joy, even when life is hard. You have a promise that persists even in the face of challenge and opposition. You have access to a Spirit who fills you to overflowing.

John 15:11 (ESV)

*These things I have spoken to you, that my joy
may be in you, and that your joy may be full.*

Acts 13:52 (NIV)

*And the disciples were filled with joy
and with the Holy Spirit.*

Prayer

Come, Holy Spirit, and fill me with your joy!

I rejoice in your presence and power in my
life. Thank you for joining me to Jesus, to his
life of service, his victory over death, and his
eternal glory!

Thank you for giving me unique gifts, gifts
that are useful to the people around me!

Thank you for the delight of your intimate
guidance and the confidence of your
prayers for me!

Let this day be a day of joyful peace for me
as I spend it reflecting on what you pour
into my life. Come, Holy Spirit, and fill me
with your joy! Amen.

Prayer Experiment: Filled up and Overflowing

Like the Secret Code Prayer from Day 13, the prayer experiment on the next page is designed to help slow down and focus your prayer time. This experiment is just more fun with color, so scrounge through your junk drawer and come back with some pencils, pens, or even crayons.

The circle at the center of the diagram on the next page represents you. Jesus pours out the Spirit on you along with all kinds of natural talents and spiritual gifts. Think of some of the things you are good at doing and that give you joy when you get to do them for others; some ways God blesses you that then end up blessing others.

Add words, colors, or repeating patterns (like waves or swirls or plus signs) to that center circle to capture just a few of the gifts and talents God has given you. As you work, imagine the Spirit pouring into your life. Prayerfully thank God for the gifts and talents you see active in your life.

Then consider how the gifts in your life joyfully overflow into the lives of people around you. Repeat the words, colors, or patterns from the central circle in the circles around you. (Of course, Jesus will pour directly into their lives as well; and Jesus also pours into and overflows you in order to bless people around you.)

One circle might represent an individual, while another could be a circle of influence, a group or institution. Take some time to pray for the people Jesus blesses through you. What other conversations with Jesus does this prayer experiment lead you into?

Combine the activity of your hand with a conversation from your heart: spend some focused prayer thanking Jesus for the overflowing Spirit and praying with joy for the people Jesus blesses through the gifts he gives to you.

Day 21, Friday

Spilled Wine

You know what they say about spilled milk. But I've never heard anyone say that you shouldn't cry over spilled *wine*. I mean, if you drop a full glass of really nice wine, what's your reaction? What a loss! What a waste! What a mess!! Maybe you don't actually cry. But maybe you want to ...

Writing to his friends in the Roman colony of Philippi, Paul uses some surprisingly Hebrew imagery. In the Old Testament, the priests sometimes had the job of pouring out a drink offering; that is, spilling fine wine over the sacrifice to make it pleasing to God.

The Greeks and Romans knew of drink offerings, too. But unlike the other gods around the ancient world, the God of Israel never needed to be fed by human offerings. The Old Testament gives us a picture of a God who wants fellowship with people; and wants to remove sin, so that eating and drinking in fellowship with God is possible.

For the joy set before him, Jesus lives out that heart of God. Jesus empties himself, pours himself out, gives his own blood as wine. Following in his master's footsteps, Paul pours himself out as a drink offering that mingles with and enhances the sacrificial offering of his friends' faith.

When you give yourself freely for the sake of people you love, when you pour yourself into the faithful sacrifice of others, when you join your self-giving love to the self-giving love of your friends, you don't experience that as loss at all.

Life might get messy, but when you live in the abundance of knowing Jesus, pouring yourself out for others doesn't bring the pain of waste or loss; that fellowship offering brings tears of joy. I guess you can cry over spilled wine.

Philippians 2:17 (NIV)

*But even if I am being poured out
like a drink offering on the sacrifice
and service coming from your faith,
I am glad and rejoice with all of you.*

Prayer

I thank you, Heavenly Father, that you have given me the ability and opportunity to pour into the lives of others.

Have I told you lately about some of my favorite people and what they are up to?

I place these people especially before your throne of grace ...

Thank you, Lord, for the people you have placed in my life. Show me how I can serve them in your name this week. Amen.

Meditation Quotation

"As we grow more fully into Christ's image, we become more fully ourselves....

As we enter more fully into our individual potency by entering into the potency of Christ's life-giving Spirit, we also enter more fully into relationship with others, more fully appreciating their own individual gifts."

—Lois Malcolm (*Holy Spirit*)

Personal Reflection

Think of three things you own that used to belong to someone else. Are these heirlooms, gifts, hand-me-downs, or ...? What feelings or memories do you associate with those objects? Make a list.

Write down three things you used to own that you freely gave to someone else. What feelings or memories do you associate with those objects? Make another list.

Day 22, Saturday

Rest and Refresh

Whew! It's been a week! Take a minute to just relax. Don't do anything at all.

Maybe you've got a to-do list that seems to be overflowing. But before you get back to all the doing, take a minute to rest in the being; take Jesus at his word of promise, and rest.

Imagine again the glass on the top of the champagne fountain. That glass is perpetually overflowing because it's connected to a perpetual source.

If you are feeling a little empty or dry today, take a moment to bring your Perpetual Source to mind. Connected to Jesus by faith, you not only have access to the refreshing water of life, that water flows perpetually through you.

Like the trickle of water Ezekiel sees flowing out of the Temple of God, down through the city of Jerusalem, down through the arid region of the Arabah, down all the way to the Dead Sea, where that living water becomes a river that transforms the wasteland into a garden, Jesus also, as the presence of God among us, pours out living water that transforms those who follow him.

As a miniature temple of the Holy Spirit, you also are connected to a Perpetual Source of life. Before you get back to all your doing, take a minute to rest in the Spirit's being—in the Spirit being present for you and filling you with refreshing, baptismal water that trickles down into the lives of the people around you.

Rest. Refresh. Whoever believes in Jesus receives a River of Life, the Spirit of Renewal, flowing from within.

John 7:38 (NIV)

[Jesus said:] "Whoever believes in me, as Scripture has said, rivers of living water will flow from within them." By this he meant the Spirit.

Ezekiel 47:9 (ESV)

And wherever the river goes, every living creature that swarms will live, and there will be very many fish. For this water goes there, that the waters of the sea may become fresh; so everything will live where the river goes.

Prayer

Come, Holy Spirit, water of life!

River flowing from Christ, God's temple among us, you fill me richly with faith and love. You are the gift of God for the tired and thirsty soul.

Refresh me and restore me as I learn to rest in you. Amen.

Day 23, Sunday

An Open Invitation

I love Philip's "evangelism method." Full of hope, and joy, and excitement at being called to follow Jesus, Philip goes to his friend Nathanael and delivers the good news. Nathanael responds not only with disbelief, but with derision: "Are you kidding me?? That's crazy!"

I think Philip could have gotten pretty defensive at that point and given some theological evidence or Bible proofs that Jesus is the Messiah. Philip could have tried to convince Negative Nate with the strength of his own personal experience. Philip could have argued, or defended, or debated, or deconstructed, or convinced, or cajoled.

I would have understood if Philip had browbeaten Nate just a little. Shoot, I would have understood if Philip had punched Nathanael in the nose .... But Philip did none of these things. In the face of outright rejection and a bad attitude, Philip extends an invitation: "Come and see."

Of course, Philip was just imitating the outreach technique of his Rabbi, who extended the same kind of invitation. But Philip's insight was profound. He didn't have to convince his friend of anything about Jesus; he just brought Nathanael to Jesus, and let Jesus take it from there.

You have a standing invitation from Jesus to wonder about what he is up to and how that affects your life. Jesus says to you again today, "Come and see."

And sometimes the best "outreach strategy" is simply to pass that invitation on to a friend who might not think very highly of religion or religious people. You don't have to convince anyone of anything. Just be like Philip being like Jesus and extend the invitation: "Come and see."

John 1:46 (NIV)

"Nazareth! Can anything good come from there?" Nathanael asked.
"Come and see," said Philip.

Prayer

Jesus, please extend your invitation to me again today. Holy Spirit, create in me a heart that wants to see what Jesus is doing in me and around me.

Jesus, please extend your invitation through me again today. Holy Spirit, give me lips that are quick to invite the people Jesus has placed around me.

When I feel under attack, Jesus—even when it feels like they are attacking you, will you please give me an open attitude and an outward focus?

Come, Holy Spirit; think in my thoughts, speak in my words, and invite through my invitation. Amen.

Watching for the Word

Sunday is a day of worship and prayer. Use this space to record something you saw, heard, read, or prayed today. What's Jesus speaking into your life?

Faith Experiment: Relationship Mapping, Part 1
On the next page you'll find just 15 verses from the first chapter of John. Notice all the invitations and relational connections. Who gets introduced to Jesus by whom? What is Jesus' response? What happens next? Draw a map or diagram or flowchart of the relationships in these verses.

John 1:35–49 (ESV)

The next day again John [the Baptist] was standing with two of his disciples, and he looked at Jesus as he walked by and said, "Behold, the Lamb of God!" The two disciples heard him say this, and they followed Jesus.

Jesus turned and saw them following and said to them, "What are you seeking?" And they said to him, "Rabbi" (which means Teacher), "where are you staying?" He said to them, "Come and you will see." So they came and saw where he was staying, and they stayed with him that day, for it was about the tenth hour.

One of the two who heard John speak and followed Jesus was Andrew, Simon Peter's brother. He first found his own brother Simon and said to him, "We have found the Messiah" (which means Christ). He brought him to Jesus. Jesus looked at him and said, "You are Simon the son of John. You shall be called Cephas" (which means Peter).

The next day Jesus decided to go to Galilee. He found Philip and said to him, "Follow me." Now Philip was from Bethsaida, the city of Andrew and Peter. Philip found Nathanael and said to him, "We have found him of whom Moses in the Law and also the prophets wrote, Jesus of Nazareth, the son of Joseph." Nathanael said to him, "Can anything good come out of Nazareth?" Philip said to him, "Come and see."

Jesus saw Nathanael coming toward him and said of him, "Behold, an Israelite indeed, in whom there is no deceit!" Nathanael said to him, "How do you know me?" Jesus answered him, "Before Philip called you, when you were under the fig tree, I saw you." Nathanael answered him, "Rabbi, you are the Son of God! You are the King of Israel!"

Faith Experiment: Relationship Mapping, Part 2

Once your map of invitational relationships in John 1 is complete, think of some people who regularly bring you closer to Jesus, and some you regularly invite to "come and see" Jesus with you. Draw a second diagram to capture some of the relationships that tie you to Jesus and to others.

Day 24, Monday

A Marginal Jesus

Jesus is at the center of our theology, the center of our faith, the center of creation! But when the eternal Son of God took on human flesh to fulfill the Father's mission in the power of the Holy Spirit, Jesus was born into a poor family who almost immediately became political refugees in a foreign country.

When the Holy Family got back from exile in Egypt, Jesus grew up in the backwater town of Nazareth in a region known as "Galilee of the Gentiles" (because it was so far from the center of religious and political power and so close to foreigners and outsiders). Peter, who also hailed from Galilee, could be picked out of a Jerusalem crowd simply by his funny *Galilean* accent.

Jesus came as an outsider, as a man on the margins. Jesus associated and *identified* with people on the wrong side of cultural and socio-economic divides. Jesus lived much like a vagrant and died just like a criminal.

After centuries of living much closer to the political and economic center of power than Jesus ever did, we as the Church can sometimes lose sight of that marginal Jesus. We will always need images and reminders of Jesus enthroned for us at the center of all power; and we also need images and reminders of the humble outcast who meets the humble and outcast right where they live.

We need the statue of Jesus, arms outstretched, towering over the city of Rio de Janeiro; and we need the sculpture of Jesus, huddled on a park bench, to all the world looking like a homeless outcast, hardly worth our notice.

Jesus is both; for us.

Matthew 26:73 (ESV)

After a little while the bystanders came up and said to Peter, "Certainly you too are one of them, for your accent betrays you."

John 1:11 (NIV)

He came to that which was his own, but his own did not receive him.

John 8:48 (ESV)

The Jews answered [Jesus], "Are we not right in saying that you are a Samaritan and have a demon?"

Prayer

Risen, ascended, and glorified Lord, look on your people with compassion.

You, who were treated as an outsider and enemy, pour out your Spirit on me so I may share your heart for the foreigner, the outsider, the marginal, and the marginalized.

Give me a heart of hospitality for people who don't look like me, or talk like me, or think like me; and make your Church a tapestry of every culture and language.

Give me your Spirit and make me more like you. Amen.

Meditation Quotation

"When the church isn't for the suffering and broken, then the church isn't for Christ. Because Jesus, with His pierced side, is always on the side of the broken."

— Ann Voskamp (*The Broken Way*)

Image Search Experiment

Do an online search for statues or paintings of a kingly Jesus, full of power and authority. You could start with the towering 100-foot-tall statue of Jesus above Rio de Janeiro (impressive, but also welcoming) and expand your search from there. Then search for images of Jesus portrayed as a foreigner or outsider. Start with the statue *Homeless Jesus* by Timothy Schmalz. Save your top three of each type.

How do you respond to those different images of Jesus? What do you find comforting or challenging about them? Which image of Jesus do you need this week?

*Bonus meditation: how did you respond to all the kitsch you saw for sale when you did your image search? What do *Homeless Jesus* coffee mugs or tote bags say about our consumer culture and our faith?

**Double bonus* meditation: the day after I composed this experiment, a bronze replica of the *Homeless Jesus* was stolen from outside a church in St. Louis, Missouri. They recovered at least part of the statue a few days later. It had already been cut down to be sold as scrap. What does *that* tell you about our consumer culture and our faith?

Day 25, Tuesday

Crossing Boundaries and Borders

Even the Samaritan woman at the well was surprised that Jesus would break with long-standing social and cultural taboos to talk to her. Who does this guy think he is?

Her fellow Samaritans were hated by the Jews and hated them right back. Though she lived far from the Temple, she knew enough Jewish religion to know that Jews considered food from the hand of a Samaritan more defiling than a pulled-pork sandwich. So why was he asking her for a drink?

Move closer to the center of religion and power and you still find people on the margin. A diminutive tax collector named Zacchaeus was living the good life in Jericho. Well, at least he was rich. But working with the Romans made him a sketchy character and earned him the label "sinner" with the religious establishment. Short on popularity and short in height, the little man had to climb a tree to see Jesus pass by. But he never expected what came next.

Why would Jesus stop to talk to *him*? Zacchaeus lived close enough to Jerusalem to know that you can't enter an unclean house without becoming unclean yourself. Why would a Rabbi insist on coming over to *his* place for dinner?

When the Son of Man came to seek and save the lost, Jesus committed to a program of crossing boundaries and borders that would certainly be offensive to anyone who knew better. But the only way to reach the ostracized, dehumanized, and marginalized is to spend time on the margins. So Jesus shows up in some surprising places to bring some surprising people into the Kingdom.

Jesus even went out of his way to find *you*, of all people! Who does this guy think he is?

Deuteronomy 10:19 (NIV)

*You are to love those who are foreigners,
for you yourselves were foreigners in Egypt.*

John 4:9 (NIV)

*The Samaritan woman said to him, "You are a
Jew and I am a Samaritan woman. How can
you ask me for a drink?"*

Luke 19:5–6 (ESV)

*Jesus said to him, "Zacchaeus, hurry and come
down, for I must stay at your house today." So he
hurried and came down and received him joyfully.*

Prayer

Come, Holy Spirit, give us the eyes of God's
compassion for a chosen people who were
once vulnerable aliens in Egypt. Move our
hearts to embody in our lives Christ's own
loving care for foreigners.

Generous Spirit, gently push us out of our
comfort zones and bring us into the lives of
people who look different from us, speak
with strange accents, or come from
different cultures.

Mold us to practice hospitality in a world
filled with people looking for friendship,
belonging, and welcoming arms. Amen.

Prayer Experiment: The Ripple Prayer

Think of all the people you see on a daily or weekly basis; people you regularly encounter in one way or another. Of course, you see or talk to friends and family, neighbors and coworkers; but other people in your regular experience are passing acquaintances, or even strangers you see regularly without even knowing their names. Jesus is with every single person in your life, both those at the center and those at the margins of your weekly experience.

Write your name in the very center circle on the next page, surrounded by the words, "Jesus is close to ..." In the next ring out, add the people who are closest to you relationally; family members or friends you see regularly.

In the next ring out, add the names of people who are important to you, but are more distant relationally. Finally, in the four corners, add the names of people on the other side of significant cultural or economic boundaries in your life. In the world you regularly inhabit, who is on the margins? You can include someone even if you don't yet know their name or their story.

There is no "wrong answer" when it comes to picking people to pray for today. Invite the Spirit to guide your selection, and don't list more than five or six people in each ring. Pray for others next time.

When you have people listed in each area, shade in the rings and corners with color as you pray for each person listed, starting with yourself.

Use the phrase, "Jesus is close to ..." as a gateway into the next ring. If you don't know what to pray for anyone on your page, simply hold them before Jesus as you add color.

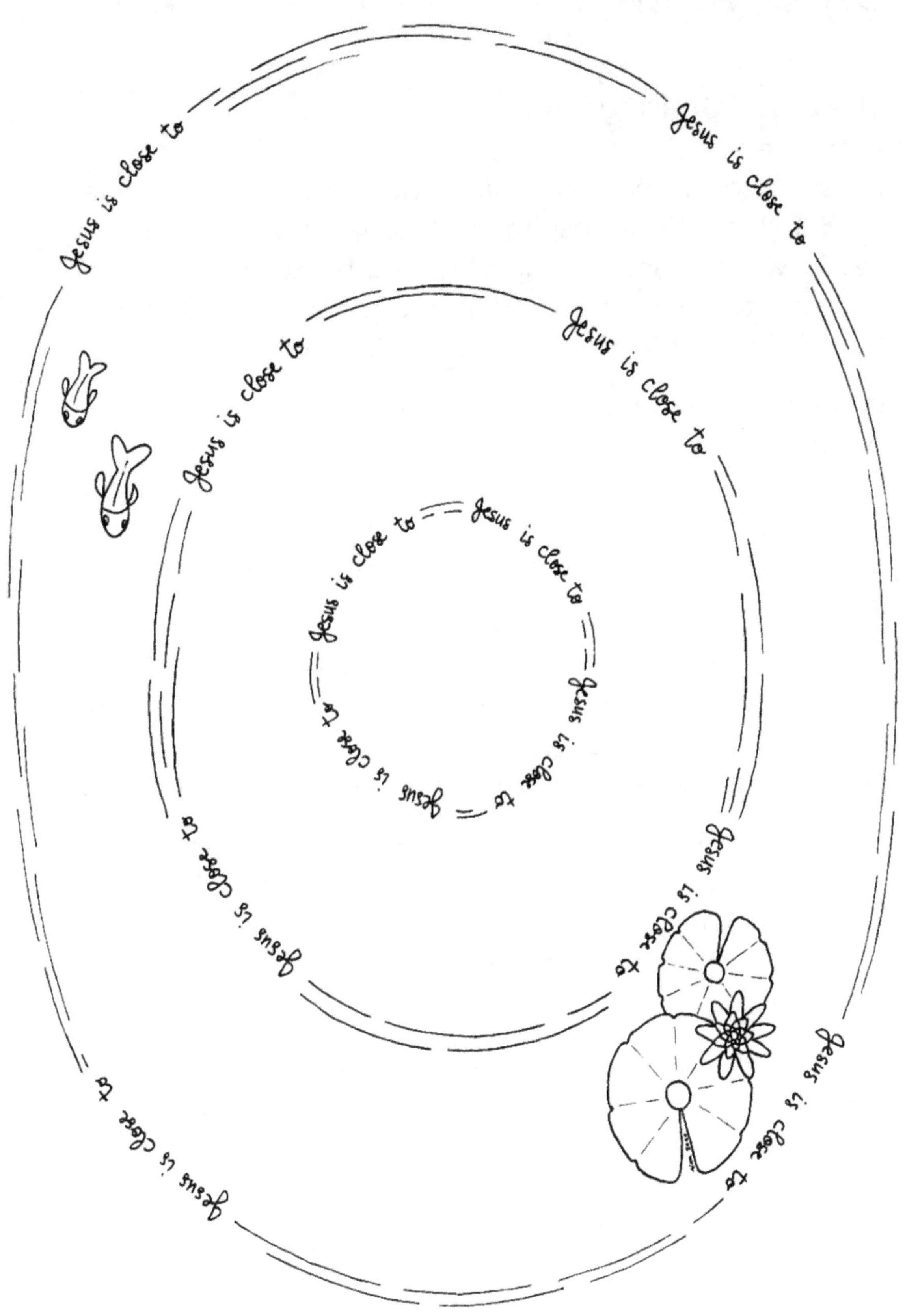

Jesus is close to
Jesus is close to
Jesus is close to
Jesus is close to
Jesus is close to
Jesus is close to
Jesus is close to
Jesus is close to
Jesus is close to
Jesus is close to
Jesus is close to
Jesus is close to
Jesus is close to

Day 26, Wednesday

The Joy of Sharing Joy

When Zacchaeus, on the margins of the crowd, suddenly finds himself at the center of attention, do you know what he does? In a fit of hospitality, Zacchaeus not only invites Jesus over for dinner, he turns his wealth into an instrument of service to outsiders and outcasts and other questionables the religious establishment tends to grumble about.

When the Samaritan woman at the well finds in Jesus the promise of living water welling up to eternal life, do you know what she does? This woman, who is so marginal she had to get water in the heat of the noonday sun, went right back into the center of her village to drag her neighbors out to meet Jesus.

Those Samaritans, outsiders themselves, in a fit of hospitality invite Jesus to come over for dinner and spend the night. And Jesus, with a heart filled to the brim for outsiders, spends two more days in that borderland village.

This pattern shows up over and over again in the story until you almost get the idea that using the weak, and hurting, and marginal, and powerless, and humble, and confused, and broken is all part of the plan.

Indeed, Jesus sees the Father's good pleasure in using unexpected people, and it fills him with a joy that can only come from the Holy Spirit. God delights to use people with sketchy track records and questionable capacity as part of a rescue mission of cosmic proportions.

Which means, of course, that *you*—with all your faults, and failures, and doubts, and disappointments—are perfectly positioned to be used by Jesus to reach the people he has put in your life. And that thought brings Jesus joy!

John 4:39 (ESV)

Many Samaritans from that town believed in him because of the woman's testimony.

Luke 10:21 (NIV)

Jesus, full of joy through the Holy Spirit, said, "I praise you, Father, Lord of heaven and earth, because you have hidden these things from the wise and learned, and revealed them to little children."

Prayer

Come, Holy Spirit, and fill me with the same joy you gave to Jesus!

I am so thankful you chose the weak and the foolish, because that means you can choose me, too!

Use me in the places I have the least power or influence. Cause me to embrace my own journey on the border between this world and the life of the world to come.

Thank you for using me to welcome strangers home into your presence. Give me the joy of expecting you to work in my life. Amen.

Meditation Quotation

"Jesus knows what it is like to be a vulnerable outsider. Raised in Nazareth of Galilee, Jesus was a marginalized Jew....

Jesus was not the right kind of Jew to be the Messiah. Jesus had an accent!

... The disciples share in their Lord's own marginality, and God surprises us by using the lowly as instruments of his salvation."

—Leopoldo A. Sánchez M. (*Sculptor Spirit*)

Personal Reflection

Have you ever thought of Jesus as someone who had an accent, who was from the "wrong side of town," or who was marginalized by other people in his culture? How does Jesus' experience as an outsider shape or change your view of him?

When have you felt most marginalized as a follower of Jesus? Are there people who make you feel like an unwelcome outsider in your regular experience?

Are there people you feel uncomfortable around because they are so different from you? What emotions do you feel in that situation, and how do you deal with them?

What promise from Jesus opens you up to other people who aren't like you?

Day 27, Thursday

Jesus Eyes

The disciples make it back to the well just in time to see a Samaritan woman going off in amazement to fetch her friends. They offer Jesus some of their Kosher Takeout, but Jesus says he has "food" they know nothing about, which causes some concern, since they are deep in enemy territory, and one does not simply eat from a street vendor if lunch can make you spiritually unclean.

But Jesus wasn't talking about *food* food. Jesus was talking about the satisfaction that comes from doing what you were designed to do: "My food is to do the delight of the one who sent me."

While the disciples are still chewing on that statement, the questionable, unclean, enemy, outsider woman shows back up, with a crowd of her closest friends. (OK; wait. She didn't have any friends, remember? She somehow went to people who looked down on her, and shamed her, and threatened her, and she told *them* about Jesus.)

Seeing the crowd, Jesus gives his disciples a new lens, a new frame, a new way of seeing and evaluating and experiencing the situation in front of them. Jesus clearly emphasizes the new kind of filter the Kingdom of God requires: "*Look*," he says, "Lift up your *eyes*; and *see*."

While the disciples have eyes to see only unclean, enemy outsiders who threaten to contaminate them, Jesus sees with new, Gospel shades. Jesus sees ripe sheaves ready and waiting to be brought in; *in*, where they belong.

See with new eyes. Trade out your old paradigm of IN vs. OUT, US vs. THEM. Pick up Jesus' metaphor and view your world through a new lens: "The fields are ripe for harvest."

John 4:35 (NIV)

Look, I tell you, lift up your eyes, and see
that the fields are white for harvest.

Prayer

Jesus, I don't see the world the way you do, and that makes me sad.

You see grain ready to be brought in with joy; I see enemies who threaten my religion.

You see people worthy of love; I see people worthy of spite.

You see strangers to welcome into the embrace of your Father; I see outsiders who don't talk like me, or dress like me, or pray like me, and that makes me uncertain, and sometimes even afraid.

Heal my eyes with your Spirit. Take away the inward focus that blinds my heart.

Forgive me and renew me, so I see people like you do. Amen.

Faith Experiment: Key Concept Calendar

Which words or images really stuck out to you this week? Take just a moment to go back and fill in some of the open spaces on your Key Concept Calendar in the back of the book. (You can find the original description of this Faith Experiment on page 28.) Keeping a daily record is helpful and looking back over a week also has its value. What did you circle or underline? Try to capture something every time you read; it could be anything!

Where Two or Three Are Gathered

Talk about one or more of the following with a friend or family member.

In the last month, where is the farthest you have been from home? In the last year? Ever?

Tell a story about a cross-cultural experience where you were the outsider, stranger, or foreigner. What was that like?

Name three people you see at least once a month who are from a different culture or background than you are. What do you know about them? How could you learn more?

Day 28, Friday

Esprit de Corps

If you've ever worked hard because you were on a team, or shared a common goal with a group, or even just had more fun because you were with your friends, then you know what it means to experience *esprit de corps.*

While that French phrase originally designated the morale of a military company, it's now commonly used for any sense of team spirit or camaraderie. *Team spirit* is actually a pretty good paraphrase, since the original translates literally as "the spirit of the body."

As followers of Jesus, we are also part of a corporate body, the Body of Christ. And the Spirit of that Body binds us together in all kinds of experiences. When one part of the Body rejoices, the Spirit binds us together in joy; when one part suffers, the Spirit enables the Body to share the load.

Sometimes, just being together as the Body is the only way we are able to express that *esprit de corps.* You embody the Spirit when you sleep next to a hospital bed, or stand vigil at a funeral luncheon, or sit quietly near someone whose heart is quietly breaking.

You might not have the right words; but you embody the Word. You share the presence of the Spirit with your presence. You show solidarity in real, physical ways, just like the One who demonstrated embodied solidarity with us by taking on flesh.

Here is the true Spirit of the Body: as you place yourself next to those who are suffering, or those who are grieving, or those who are marginalized or oppressed, you are acting in the Spirit of Jesus. You are functioning as the Body of Christ, participating in the mystery of *esprit de corps.*

Hebrews 13:3 (ESV)

Remember those who are in prison,
as though in prison with them,
and those who are mistreated,
since you also are in the body.

Prayer

Loving Father, open my heart to people around me who carry burdens, who struggle, who face needs beyond their means to provide.

Give me a heart of compassion and a spirit of solidarity. Show me how I can bear their burdens in concrete ways.

Accept my prayers for their present as well as their future. I hold before you today people I know are struggling this week, especially ...

Pour out your Spirit and be present in the midst of their struggles. Give them hope; give them courage; give them peace, all for the sake of Jesus. Amen.

Day 29, Saturday

A Covenant of Rest

Against my personal expectation and personal patterns, the Jewish day begins at sunset. I feel like I've known that fact, gleaned from church as well as popular culture, for a long time. But I don't often think about the ramifications.

I mean, imagine living in a habitual routine where one of the first things you had to get done today was get ready for bed! How would it change your experience, if you started your daily agenda with *rest*, and only later, work?

That pattern of rest *then* work dates back to the very beginning. The Jewish week began on Sunday, the first day of creation, but if you go back to Genesis and track that first week, you'll come to a startling realization: human beings don't show up until right before the very first Sabbath, the day of rest!

It's true! Created in the image of God and commissioned to tend the Garden and participate in God's creative work, the very first thing these humans do is take a day off!

That day of rest is so important to God that it becomes a covenant, a sign of the relationship between the Almighty God who rested on the sixth day and the people whom God dearly loves.

God's people rest in order to get to know their Creator better. God's people rest to enjoy the promise of covenant love and mercy. God's people rest in order to faithfully fulfill one of their most important callings: to be completely dependent on their Maker and Redeemer.

Your day might not start with sundown. Your job might not begin with vacation. But you are completely dependent on Jesus. Before you work at anything else, rest in his promises.

Exodus 31:16–17 (NIV)

The Israelites are to observe the Sabbath, celebrating it for the generations to come as a lasting covenant. It will be a sign between me and the Israelites forever, for in six days the LORD made the heavens and the earth, and on the seventh day he rested and was refreshed.

Prayer

Come, Lord Jesus, and give me your rest.

Amen.

Day 30, Sunday

Divine CPR

The Creation follows a certain rhythm of night and day, evening and morning, seedtime, harvest, and fallow fields. As created beings, humans also have a God-given rhythm of rest, and work, and even play; times of recuperation, times of production, times of recreation.

Like all the best parts of God's original design, that rhythm has been twisted and defaced by sin. Fallen humans suffer from a kind of spiritual arrhythmia: our hearts no longer beat in time with God's heart, and our lives careen out of control from one extreme to the next. We lack a God-given rhythm of grace.

Jesus came to restore all that was lost and twisted by sin. The New Creation will see the final fulfillment of God's good gifts; then we will know fully the blessings of rest, and work, and play. (The New Creation isn't endless, pointless, directionless vacation days; your work will no longer be a curse, but you will have plenty to do!)

You have that future promise. And Jesus shows up in your present, fallen reality to begin to set things right. Jesus performs a divine kind of CPR to give you new life.

Did you ever learn what "CPR" stands for? Cardio- (heart) pulmonary (lungs) Resuscitation (bring back to life). By breathing the Spirit into our deadened lives, Jesus sets our hearts back in synch with God's heart. Our arrhythmia is replaced with a rhythm of grace. Rest, work, and play all become places we can give glory to God; places we see the Spirit at work; places we get to know Jesus better.

Come, Holy Spirit! Breathe into our failing lungs and make our hearts beat in rhythm with God's grace! Amen.

1 Corinthians 5:17 (NIV)

Therefore, if anyone is in Christ, the new creation has come: The old has gone, the new is here!

Psalm 104:30 (ESV)

When you send forth your Spirit, they are created, and you renew the face of the ground.

Prayer

Heavenly Father, Creator God, I stand in awe of the beauty, variety, and splendor your creation displays!

Then I look at my own life, and I see the ways I can distort your good gifts. I experience such small joy in my rest; I take such little pride in my work; I regularly ignore your presence in my play.

Loving Father, heal the broken rhythm of my life. Send your Holy Spirit to shape me more and more like Jesus, and his constant connection to you.

Teach me to know you through my rest.
Teach me to know you through my work.
Teach me to know you through my play.
Amen.

Watching for the Word

Sunday is a day of worship and prayer. Use this space to record something you saw, heard, read, or prayed today. What's Jesus speaking into your life?

Personal Reflection

If someone who didn't know you looked at your calendar this week, month, or year, what would they learn about you and your priorities?

What does your pattern of rest look like? When in your week do you interact with prayer, worship, or God's Word?

What kind of work do you find most fulfilling and why? How does the way you spend the largest part of most of your days align with the way God has uniquely gifted you?

When do you get a chance to be playful? In what ways do you experience creativity? How do you see God at work in the ways you choose to play?

Day 31, Monday

Breakfast with Jesus

John 21 has to be one of my favorite chapters in the whole Bible! It's after the resurrection but before Pentecost, and Peter and his companions still don't know what to do with themselves. So Peter says, "I'm going fishing!" Good call, Peter.

Without any clear direction, these fishermen go back to doing what they know best, with the same kind of success we have come to expect (which is to say, none). After a long night with no fish in the boat, the morning dawns on a stranger who tells them to cast their nets on the other side. We've seen a version of this scene before, so we're not surprised when the result is a miraculous catch of fish!

Part of what I love about this scene is that Jesus seems so *playful*. The disciples don't recognize him right away, and Jesus just plays along. But the next part is even better. The risen Jesus, Lord of Heaven and Earth, King of the Universe, One with the Father from eternity and to eternity, has been busy *making his friends some breakfast*. Jesus has fish on the Weber and bread in the oven.

And then—*guys!*—then Jesus says: "Bring some of the fish *you just caught.*" Sure, the disciples "caught" the fish, but only because Jesus was there, doing his thing! But Jesus acts like their work is meaningful and important. This glorified Savior humbles himself to receive what his followers bring to the table, even though they couldn't have brought it without him.

That's the dynamic of the life of following. Jesus beautifully and gently brings Peter back into that relationship right after that breakfast. Jesus invites you into that relationship again today. Jesus blesses and enables your work, and then receives with joy whatever you bring to the table.

John 21:10–12, 22 (ESV)

Jesus said to them, "Bring some of the fish that you have just caught."

So Simon Peter went aboard and hauled the net ashore, full of large fish, 153 of them. And although there were so many, the net was not torn.

Jesus said to them, "Come and have breakfast." … Jesus said to [Peter], "… You follow me!"

Prayer

Jesus, you amaze me! I love how you invite your followers into a deeper relationship with you.

I love that, even as the Resurrected Lord, you delight in making a campfire breakfast of fish and pita bread for your disciples on the beach. I love that you call them from their nets again, with another surprising and abundant catch.

Lord, give me your Spirit of service, your Spirit of abundance, your Spirit of creation and recreation. Teach me to delight in everyday moments of rest, work, and play. And never stop inviting me to break bread with you. Amen.

Meditation Quotation

"All you really have is your willingness to fail, coupled with the mountain of evidence that the Maker has never left nor forsaken you....

I'm pleasantly expendable, delightfully unnecessary. We're not invited into this because God needs us, but because he *wants* us."

—Andrew Peterson *(Adorning the Dark)*

Faith Experiment: An Abbreviation Prayer

CPR stands for Cardiopulmonary Resuscitation.

INRI, nailed above Jesus' head on the cross, stood for "Jesus of Nazareth, King of the Jews." Some early versions of the Greek New Testament use the abbreviations XS for Christ, STS for cross, PAP for Father, and PNA for Spirit.

VDMA is an abbreviation of a phrase that means "The Word of the Lord endures forever," just like DV stands for, "God willing." J.S. Bach was known to start his compositions with JJ (Jesus, help!) and end them with SDG (To God alone be glory!)

Use some of those abbreviations or make up your own to write out a short prayer on a 3x5 card, or even the back of a business card. See how many abbreviations you can fit into a single paragraph.

(Extra bonus points for using "NASA.")

Day 32, Tuesday

Exhausted and Overwhelmed

Have you ever tried to find the Bible verse that says God won't give you more than you can handle? It's not an easy task, especially because *the Bible doesn't say that.*

Oh, there's the verse about God not allowing you to be tempted beyond what you can bear (1 Cor. 10:13); God knows you and loves you and won't let temptation arise in your life that is "more than you can handle." But that's not exactly the same thing ...

In fact, there are times when God actually allows life in general to be such a burden that you are overwhelmed; times you actually *do* have more than you can handle; times you come to the end of your rope. At those times, your dependence on Jesus becomes a beautifully clear and present reality in your life.

If you feel exhausted and overwhelmed, don't add the burden of trying to live up to an imaginary ideal of "never having more than you can handle." God's people are completely overwhelmed sometimes; that's a normal and expected part of the faith journey.

When you have more than you could possibly handle, Jesus is right there with you. When you are overwhelmed beyond your ability to endure, even when your burden is so heavy it feels like you are going to die, you are invited to trust the God who raises the dead. When you come to the end of your rope, you find Jesus waiting for you there.

It's OK to be overwhelmed. It's OK to feel like you have more than you can handle. (You probably do.)

And Jesus is right there with you, no matter what.

Matthew 11:28 (NIV)

Come to me, all you who are weary and burdened, and I will give you rest.

2 Corinthians 1:8–9 (ESV)

For we were so utterly burdened beyond our strength that we despaired of life itself. Indeed, we felt that we had received the sentence of death. But that was to make us rely not on ourselves but on God who raises the dead.

Prayer

Jesus, I need you today.

I need you in my moments of exhaustion. I need you in my moments of stress. I need you when the burden seems like more than I can bear.

Be present for me today, Jesus. Give me the rest you have promised. Refresh me with your Spirit. Empower me with your Word. Renew me with your strength.

Jesus, I need you. Teach me to need you more and more. Amen.

Day 33, Wednesday

God Delights in Play

In Proverbs 8, we find God delighting in Lady Wisdom at the very beginning of creation, and Lady Wisdom taking playful delight in God and in the inhabitants of creation.

That "playful delight" also marks the restoration of creation: boys and girls will be laughing and playing in the streets, and just plain having fun. Rejoicing with playful delight is the new status quo of the New Creation.

You serve a God who made the blue whale as well as the platypus. You have a Savior who turned gallons and gallons *and gallons* of water set aside for following strict religious rules into more of the best wine than could be drunk in a month full of weddings. You have received a Spirit who blows playfully, like the wind.

Play, like rest, is an act of trust: trust that your ongoing work is not necessary to keep the planet spinning. God likes play. God created play. God loves it when you play, in part because you can't be worried about everything else if you are enjoying God's good gifts with delight.

As a human being, you were created in the image of God. You therefore have a calling to image God to the rest of creation. You certainly do that in your labor, as a steward of God's creation; you also image God in your play, as you delight in God's creation.

When you receive them with delight, and in dependence on Jesus, your rest, your work, and your play all move you into deeper relationship with God, your Creator, Redeemer, and Sustainer.

And that makes God rejoice with playful delight!

Proverbs 8:27, 30–31 (ESV)

When [God] established the heavens,
I [Wisdom] was there ...

I was daily his delight, rejoicing before him
always, rejoicing in his inhabited world and
delighting in the children of man.

Zechariah 8:5 (NIV)

The city streets will be filled with boys and girls
playing there.

Prayer

Your work is amazing, God! I praise you for the magnificence, multiplicity, and majesty of your creative work!

Let my own recreation imitate your creative power. As I play, let my joy echo your own.

As I am refreshed by time spent in fun, be present in my leisure. Glory to you, O Lord! Amen.

Meditation Quotation

"Finding a place for play in our lives reminds us that it is salutary to stand still before God amid the busyness of life and behold his creation. Making room for *fiesta* allows us to embrace our creatureliness by rejoicing in and making use of God's created gifts simply because they are beautiful and wonderful even in the midst of a world so full of pain and suffering."

—Leopoldo A. Sánchez M. (*Sculptor Spirit*)

Faith Experiment: Just for Fun

Do something today just for the fun of it. Make sure it doesn't accomplish anything on your to-do list. Pick up a musical instrument you haven't played in years or dig that old ball out of the basement or garage. Pull your old watercolor set from the back of that drawer or dance around your living room.

Feel free to invite a friend, but only if they are willing to have fun and not get anything productive done.

If that's too much to ask for a Wednesday, don't feel bad. Look at your calendar over the next couple of weeks and find at least one 30–60-minute slot you can schedule for nothing but play. Think of it as an experiment in mental health and productivity. But whatever you do, don't take it too seriously! Just have some fun.

Day 34, Thursday

Too Much of a Good Thing

Even good gifts make lousy gods. But somehow our natural, fallen tendency is to take any divine gift and immediately set up an altar to supplant the Giver.

Rest is a gift God intends as a blessing. We can get too much of that good thing, until we reject God's other gifts because the couch is so comfy and Netflix so easy to binge. Or we can place our hope in rest: if only I could take a vacation, *then* my life would be good! You don't have to burn incense to your pillow: whatever you place your hope in becomes your god.

Work can be like that, too. God intends work as a blessing; sin turns work into a curse. We can gorge ourselves on too much work, taking pride in our 80-hour week. Or we can turn work into an idol: if only I had more work, *then* my life would be good, and my dreams would come true!

Not surprisingly, play is another good gift that makes a lousy god. Our play is often self-centered and self-indulgent. Our culture equates *fun* with *sin*. Much of what we do to "let off a little steam" you wouldn't invite Jesus to do with you. And if Jesus isn't welcome, what does that say about our "fun"?

We can turn rest, work, and play—all good gifts from God—into burdens as well as idols. We can literally rest, work, or play our bodies and our souls to death.

Into that mess steps Jesus, who finds the time to rest in the Spirit, and rejoices in doing the work of the Father, and delights in the people around him. Jesus is the Good Gift that supplants all the idols in your life. Jesus gives you the gift of the Spirit, who opens your heart to receive rest, work, and play with thanksgiving, and use them to your good and to God's glory. Jesus is the Gift who restores to us the Giver.

Genesis 3:17 (NIV)

Cursed is the ground because of you; through painful toil you will eat food from it all the days of your life.

Amos 6:1, 6–7 (NIV)

Woe to you who are complacent in Zion...
You drink wine by the bowlful and use the finest lotions, but you do not grieve over the ruin of Joseph. Therefore you will be among the first to go into exile; your feasting and lounging will end.

Prayer

Come, Creator Spirit, convict me of my sin. Show me the ways my attitude or actions distort your good creation. Help me see how my routine has grown imbalanced, unfulfilling, or even idolatrous.

Come, Sculptor Spirit, renew in me a rhythm of experiencing your presence in my rest, in my work, and in my play.

Rescue me from sloth and refresh me with your peace. Save me from painful toil and give me joy in my daily calling. Preserve me from self-serving leisure and cause me to receive the gift of fun with true joy.

Forgive me, renew me, and lead me, so I may delight in your will and walk in your ways, to the glory of your holy name. Amen.

Faith Experiment: The Secret Code Prayer

You met the Secret Code Prayer back on page 50. Give it another try today as you spend some focused time in confession. Prayerfully consider your daily, weekly rhythm of rest, work, and play. Where is that rhythm out of whack?

Confess the ways you abuse or ignore rest, work, or play in your life. Admit your self-centered habits and routines. Be specific. You can be totally honest; even if someone else sees this page by mistake, a passing glance won't give anything away.

Here's a reminder on how this prayer experiment works:

1) Set a timer for five minutes.

2) Write out your prayer of confession, one letter in each box of the graph card on the next page.

Choose all UPPER- or all lowercase letters, don't add spaces between words or use punctuation, and don't worry about spelling. (Use some abbreviations from Day 31 if you want.)

Don't feel like you have to get the whole thing done in five minutes or less; just spend the time in focused prayer.

3) When the timer goes off, finish your thought, add an Amen, and stop.

4) Reread what you wrote, slowly praying once more.

5) Close with a prayer for forgiveness: "Forgive me, renew me, and lead me, so I may delight in your will and walk in your ways, to the glory of your holy name."

Then go about your routine in confident joy. Jesus forgives your sins, breathes new life into your lungs, and makes your heart beat in rhythm with God's grace!

Day 35, Friday

I Got Rhythm!

I grew up with *The Muppet Show*, and I clearly remember a scene where Fozzie Bear sings his rendition of "I Got Rhythm!" Fozzie obviously *doesn't* have any rhythm, and that's what makes the shtick funny. By the end of the scene, Fozzie's accompanist, Rowlf the Dog, changes the score to read, "I *ain't* got rhythm!" Fozzie, blissfully ignorant, sings along. Wocka wocka!

My kids grew up with *Phineas and Ferb*, and I clearly remember an episode where the title characters are trying to get the drummer from *Love Händel* to come out of retirement for one last gig. The drummer, now working as a librarian, complains that he's lost the beat. In fact, he comically sings, "I ain't got rhythm," all the while creating a wicked groove with library books and a date stamp without knowing it. Funny. Like Fozzie, but in reverse.

Sometimes, in the course of your ordinary, everyday routine, it's hard to tell when you've got a healthy rhythm of rest, work, and play, and when this world's arrhythmia has infected your heart. Sometimes, you get to be Rowlf and make some minor adjustments to accommodate a friend who doesn't have very good rhythm right now, and just can't see it for themselves. And sometimes you get to play the role of Phineas and Ferb, and help someone see that they have gotten into a groove without even noticing.

The body of Christ works like that: we put up with each other, and accommodate each other, and encourage each other, all the while knowing that others will have to put up with our own arrhythmia in one way or another. Each of us can lose the beat from time to time, but in the Spirit, we can still "make beautiful music together." (Wocka wocka!)

Ephesians 4:2–3 (NIV)

Be completely humble and gentle; be patient, bearing with one another in love. Make every effort to keep the unity of the Spirit through the bond of peace.

Prayer

Heavenly Father, thank you for the people you have put around me! For all their faults and failings, they are a beautiful gift you have given me!

Lord Jesus, give me your heart of compassion for those whose imbalanced lives bump up against my own imbalances.

Make me eager to overlook minor irritations and quick to forgive unintended slights.

Come, Holy Spirit, and strengthen our bond of peace. Today, I pray for people in my faith family I tend to have trouble getting along with, especially ...

Make us all more humble and gentle, more patient and peaceful. Make us all more like Jesus, in whose name I pray. Amen.

Meditation Quotation

"You're kidding me, right? Y-you're kidding me.
Don't you see what you were doing right then?
That's a wicked groove you were starting to
move. Mister, you got rhythm times ten!"

—Phineas Flynn (*Ain't Got Rhythm*)

Where Two or Three Are Gathered

Set aside some time to walk through the following
conversation with a friend or family member.

Describe a time when you felt well rested and refreshed.

*Describe a time when you were really proud of the work
you did or something you accomplished.*

What do you do for fun?

Day 36, Saturday

Keep Beginning With Rest

We began this discipleship travel log way back on Day 1 with rest. Do you remember? Did it seem odd to start by not doing anything? Day 1 set an intentional pattern, and now you know why: the rhythm of rest, work, and play begins with *rest*.

Keep doing that. Keep beginning your projects completely dependent on Jesus. Keep trusting that God is in control even when you are snoring on the couch.

Don't forget work! And certainly, don't forget play!! But hold onto that idea that the most important thing you can do is trust. Let God be God.

Resting first means you aren't in control or responsible for the final outcome. You don't have to own every detail or determine the outcome. Resting first allows you to fully engage your work and your play, as well.

Today begins the last week of this travel log. We start this week the way we started at the very beginning of this travel log: go take a nap!

Psalm 127:2 (NIV)

Unless the LORD builds the house,
  the builders labor in vain.
Unless the LORD watches over the city,
  the guards stand watch in vain.

In vain you rise early and stay up late,
toiling for food to eat—for [the LORD] grants
sleep to those he loves.

Psalm 4:8 (NIV)

In peace I will lie down and sleep, for you
alone, LORD, make me dwell in safety.

Prayer

Lord, I thank you for the gift of safety and
the gift of sleep.

As I think of people in my life who struggle
to find safety or sleep, friends or family who
are busy, anxious, or stressed to the point of
exhaustion, I ask you to pour out your Spirit
of peace and rest on them.

I pray especially for ...

Give my friends and family the gift of
confident sleep. Refresh them and renew
them, Lord. Amen.

Day 37, Sunday

Pour out Your Spirit!

In Acts 2, Peter says that the risen and ascended Christ has poured out the Spirit at Pentecost. In John 14, Jesus says he will ask, and the Father will send the Spirit. In John 20, Jesus breathes the Spirit on his disciples. In Luke 11, Jesus says the Father will give the Spirit to all those who ask.

In the Nicene Creed, we confess the Spirit who "proceeds from the Father and the Son; who with the Father and the Son together is worshiped and glorified." The Church throughout the ages has prayed and sung, "Come, Holy Spirit!" Jesus says, in John 3, that the Spirit is like the wind, and the wind blows wherever it wants.

One of the great mysteries of the Trinity is this: you cannot separate the Father, Son, and Spirit in their outward activity. You can say *the Father* raised Jesus from the dead, *or the Spirit* raised Jesus from the dead, or *Jesus* rose from the dead: all are equally true. You can say *the Father* sends the Spirit, *the Son* pours out the Spirit, or *the Spirit* blows like the wind: all are equally true.

Don't let that mystery of the Trinity discourage or confuse your prayers! The point is this: the Spirit is sent to *you*; poured out on *you*; willingly comes to *you!*

Ask the Father to send the Spirit, and trust that the Father gives the Spirit to all who ask. Pray to Jesus to pour out his Spirit, and trust that Pentecost is still happening today. Invite the Spirit to blow into your heart, and watch the Spirit kindle faith, and trust, and dependence on Jesus.

Pray early and often for the Spirit. Pray to the Father. Pray to the Son. Pray to the Spirit. And trust the activity of the Trinity that brings the Spirit into your life.

Luke 11:13 (NIV)

How much more will your Father in heaven give the Holy Spirit to those who ask!

Prayer

Holy God, you made me your child in my baptism. You committed yourself to hearing my prayers. You promised to give your Holy Spirit to those who ask.

So I pray in confidence: Father, give me your Spirit! Jesus, pour out your Spirit on me! Come, Holy Spirit!

When guilt burdens my heart, Father, give me your Spirit! When I am under attack, Jesus, pour out your Spirit! When I seek to serve others, come, Holy Spirit!

When I encounter strangers, Father, give me your Spirit! When I go to rest, or work, or play, Jesus, pour out your Spirit!

Come, Holy Spirit! Do not leave me on my own to fend for myself, but bind me to the life, death, and resurrection of my Lord, Jesus Christ and bring me into his fellowship with the Father. Amen.

Watching for the Word

It's Sunday again! Use this space to write down or sketch something you saw, heard, read, or prayed. What's the Spirit got for you today?

Day 38, Monday

Trying on Your New Glasses

Over the last five weeks we have explored five different ways of talking about and understanding the work of the Holy Spirit in the life of believers. Focused on how the Spirit shapes our lives to resonate with the life of Jesus, we've followed these five themes:

(1) Renewal: Daily dying and rising in baptism.
The Spirit who raised Jesus from the dead shapes Jesus' death and resurrection in us. We daily walk in the waters of our own baptism, drowning our old, sinful, selfish nature and rising daily to new life.

(2) Spiritual Warfare: Struggle and temptation.
Jesus faced the tempter in the desert and in the Garden; the Spirit shapes in us Jesus' dependence on God's Word in the face of trial and temptation.

(3) Pouring: Filled up and overflowing to others.
Just as Jesus received the Spirit and then poured himself out in service for others, so we receive the Spirit from Jesus and overflow into the lives of the people around us.

(4) Hospitality: A heart for outsiders.
The Spirit led Jesus to encounter people on the margins; the Spirit shapes in us Jesus' heart of welcome for the marginal and marginalized.

(5) Rhythm: A pattern of rest, work, and play.
Just as Jesus knew work, rest, and refreshment in the Spirit, so we find a Spirit-led rhythm of rest, work, and play.

Now it's time to put those models of seeing the Holy Spirit to work, as if you were trying on new glasses. Each set of lenses will help you see something unique, and each perspective helps you understand the whole. Let's begin.

Scripture Experiment: Rereading Pentecost

Acts chapter 2 records the events of the Day of Pentecost. That story takes 47 verses, and we can't reproduce them all here. So grab a Bible you feel comfortable writing in, or print out all of Acts 2 (on three pages), and let's get to work.

Your job is to read through Acts 2:1–47 carefully and prayerfully with our five lenses or ways of seeing the work of the Spirit in mind. (You could come up with other models or ways of talking, but for practice, just stick with the five we have covered in this travel log.)

Look for vocabulary words or images that evoke these different models for the work of the Spirit in the life of Jesus as well as in your own life. Use a different color to highlight or underline the different ways the Spirit works.

(1) Use purple to highlight talk of dying and rising; that's the Renewal model.

(2) Use Red to capture language of battles or conflict or victory; that's the Spiritual Warfare model.

(3) Blue is a good color for the Pouring model, since water is poured out and overflows; any talk of filling or pouring or receiving can be marked with blue.

(4) Try using Orange to identify people who are marginal or marginalized to help you see the Hospitality model.

(5) Finally, use Green to highlight any Rhythm that sticks out to you; patterns of worship, work, rest, or play.

Pro Tip: Do (1) last. Although the Renewal Model may be the most familiar, it's the least represented in Acts 2. Invoke the Holy Spirit, then carefully read through the text several times. I'll show you some of what I found on the next page. (No peeking!) [Well, OK; peek if it's helpful....]

Scripture Experiment: Some Preliminary Results

Going back to Acts 2 in light of the main themes of this travel log, here are some of the things that stuck out to me.

(1) Renewal (Purple): Daily dying and rising in baptism.
This one was a bit of a challenge! Acts 2:23–24 talks about Jesus' *death* and *resurrection*. (So does verse 32.) And verse 38 uses the vocabulary of *baptism*, *repentance*, and *forgiveness*—all key Renewal model vocabulary words.

(2) Spiritual Warfare (Red): Struggle and temptation.
Conflict, victory, warning, enemies, and the language of saving all fit Spiritual Warfare. I marked verses 20–21, 35, and 40 especially.

(3) Pouring (Blue): Filled up and overflowing to others.
The language of pouring or filling was explicit in a few verses (4, 17–18, 33). It's funny: of all the ways I traditionally think of Pentecost, "pouring" is not high on my list. But it seems to be a central theme in Acts 2!

(4) Hospitality (Orange): A heart for outsiders.
Verses 5–13 nicely set up the mission to and through the marginalized: these are people from every nation hearing from marginal Galileans. Verse 39 also fits.

(5) Rhythm (Green): A pattern of rest, work, and play.
Acts 2 begins and ends with a regular pattern of rest and worship. In verse 1, the disciples all gather in one place *because it is the day of Pentecost.* This annual celebration of harvest was part of the rhythm of rest and worship God built into the pattern of seasons and festivals. By the end of the chapter, we find the growing number of Jesus-followers devoted to regular patterns of spiritual discipline, like the breaking of bread and prayer.

Acts 2:1 (NIV)

When the day of Pentecost came,
they were all together in one place.

Prayer

Come, Holy Spirit, shape the rhythm of my
days, my weeks, and my years.

Give me times of planting, times of harvest,
and times of feasting and celebration.

Increase in me a delight in your presence
and a desire for your Word.

Shape times and seasons to point me back
to your work in this world. Give me fellow
followers of Jesus to share in my burdens as
well as my joys.

Lord of Pentecost, harvest, and celebration,
gather, empower, renew, and send out your
people! Amen.

Hymn Verse Prayer

Come, Holy Ghost, God and Lord,
With all Your graces now outpoured
On each believer's mind and heart;
Your fervent love to them impart.
Lord, by the brightness of Your light
In holy faith Your Church unite;
From every land and every tongue
This to Your praise, O Lord, our God, be sung:
Alleluia! Alleluia!

Lutheran Service Book, 497
Text: Martin Luther

Where Two or Three Are Gathered

Talk about one or more of the following with a friend or family member.

What's the best party you go to every year?

What's the best worship experience you go to every year?

Where is your favorite place to go on vacation? Where did you go on vacation growing up?

Go back to your Scripture Experiment from Acts 2 and compare notes. How did you respond to this activity? What was your biggest takeaway?

Day 39, Tuesday

What's Your Next Step?

Yesterday you looked at the story of Pentecost in Acts 2 through the lens of five different ways of seeing the work of the Spirit. Today you get to pick up those same lenses and look at the work of the Spirit in your own life.

If you have been adding to the Key Concept Calendar in the back of this book, review what you have written or drawn. Which of the first five weeks seemed to impact you most? What stands out to you?

Then think about the work of the Holy Spirit in your life. Which one of the following resonates most?

(1) Renewal: Daily dying and rising in baptism.
(2) Spiritual Warfare: Struggle and temptation.
(3) Pouring: Filled up and overflowing to others.
(4) Hospitality: A heart for outsiders.
(5) Rhythm: A pattern of rest, work, and play.

How do you see these activities of the Spirit at work in you and in your life right now?

Sometimes following Jesus feels like taking a huge step into the unknown. Sometimes you are actually called to make a significant and immediate change.

And most of the time, following Jesus is more like finding a small next step, and taking it. Move forward. Run a small experiment. See where it leads. Those small steps can add up to some pretty significant changes over time.

As you look for what the Spirit is doing in your life, don't try to run in five different directions all at once. What *one* thing is the Spirit doing in your life right now? What small next step is Jesus inviting you to take?

How would you pray based on these different ways of viewing the Spirit's activity in your life?

What different promises do these different activities of the Spirit speak into your life?

Which *one* way of understanding the Spirit's work do you need right now in order to take a next step?

For the Record

Here's another way of thinking about those Personal Reflection questions:

- What's Jesus speaking into your life?
- What response is Jesus shaping in you?
- What promise is guiding your next step?

If you don't know how to begin answering any (or all) of those questions, take that as an invitation from Jesus to pray for the Sprit and keep your eyes open to what Jesus is doing in your life.

Needing Jesus is the single most important trait of any disciple. Jesus won't give up on you.

Now record your next step on the next page.

Whether you have a clear direction or only a vague inkling of a next step, try to put something down in each section. Writing down your next step will help you take it.

If you just don't know what step to take or who in your life might be there to help you take it, that's OK. If you can't come up with a promise from Jesus to guide your next step, go back through your notes in this book and see what sticks out to you.

You aren't doing it wrong if you have trouble filling in any of the blanks. Chances are the trouble you are having is an indication that Jesus is up to something in your life.

Pray, "Come, Holy Spirit!" and wonder with Jesus about how he might fill in those blanks with you. Spending time praying or talking to a friend about not knowing your next step can be a really great next step!

My Next Step:

I'll take this step with the help of these people
On My Rope:

The Promise from Jesus
that guides my next step is:

Day 40, Wednesday

Sculptor Spirit

The same Spirit who filled Jesus now fills you, and shapes your life to echo, mirror, and even resemble the life of Christ.

The Spirit shapes the death and resurrection of Jesus in your life as you daily die to sin and rise to New Creation life, even ahead of the resurrection. One day, the Spirit will raise you to eternal life, just as the Spirit raised Jesus.

The Spirit shapes in you the struggle and testing of Jesus in the wilderness and Garden. The Spirit clothes you with armor and protects you from assault. The Spirit shapes the "*Abba*, Father" prayer Jesus prayed in Gethsemane on your lips, too: *Father, not my will, but your delight be done.*

Just as Jesus received and then poured out the Spirit, now the Spirit fills you to overflowing, so that you also pour yourself out in joyful service for others.

The Spirit shapes Jesus' heart of hospitality for outsiders in you, so that your life reflects the open invitation of Jesus to all those around you, especially to those on the margins.

The Spirit shapes a rhythm of rest, work, and play in you; a pattern Jesus lived out in his own earthly life; a rhythm intended to help you get to know Jesus better.

In all of these ways, and more, the Sculptor Spirit shapes and molds and conforms your life to the image of Christ for the sake of others.

When that sculpting doesn't feel safe or comfortable, remember that the Spirit has all the necessary skill and the perfect design to work from. The Sculptor Spirit is shaping you into a unique and beautiful work of art.

Come, Holy Spirit! Make me like Jesus. Amen.

Psalm 138:8 (ESV)

*The LORD will fulfill his purpose for me;
your steadfast love, O LORD, endures forever.
Do not forsake the work of your hands.*

Prayer

Come, Holy Spirit, renew me again today.

Where my will is weak, strengthen me. Where my resolve has wavered, restore me. Where my patterns of dependence on Jesus have come unraveled, reestablish your rhythm in my life.

Sculptor Spirit, you shape me to be more like Jesus. Do not abandon the work of your hands. Join me to Jesus' death, and raise me with Jesus to resurrection life.

Form in me his trusting in the wilderness. Mold in me his heart for outsiders. Fill me with your presence, even as you filled him.

Come, Holy Spirit, conform my present and my future to the abundant life of my Jesus. Amen.

Something to Share

We follow Jesus better when we follow him together. We all have something to learn, and something to share.

Find one thing that made a difference in your life over the last 40 days and share it with a friend.

Maybe it was a specific thought or Scripture verse. Maybe it was a prayer experiment or a new way of imagining the work of the Spirit. Maybe the time you set aside in God's presence helped you see something you had forgotten or had never seen before.

Take any one thing—one thought, experiment, reading, or prayer—that had an impact on you, and share it with someone else. Try to express why it was meaningful for you. Invite them to run an experiment and see if it might be meaningful for them, too.

By sharing even one thing with someone else, you plant that Word deeper in your own heart and life. You also extend an invitation for someone else to begin to wonder what the Spirit is up to in their life, as well.

Following Jesus can be scary and exciting and difficult and rewarding; and it's just more fun when you share the experience with others.

We follow Jesus better when we follow him together. Feel free to share your insight or your story of what the Spirit is shaping in you with the Next Step Community by emailing us at Curator@findmynextstep.org.

When you share your story of taking a next step, you help someone else take theirs.

What I shared:

Who I shared it with:

How it went:

About Next Step Press

Our Mission

Next Step Press cultivates individuals, leaders, and communities that infuse collaboration, innovation, and delight into the perpetual adventure of following Jesus. As part of that mission, we create resources that equip and encourage next-step discipleship and support a culture of delight-driven discipleship growth.

Other Resources from Next Step Press

If this resource encouraged and equipped your faith walk, you might check out the following.

- *Delight! Discipleship as the Adventure of Loving and Being Loved.*

This award-winning book from Justin Rossow helps you find renewed joy in the life of following Jesus.

- *Ponder Anew: A Hymn Journal of Trust and Confidence*

Featuring illustrations from Visual Faith™ Ministry artists, this unique resource combines music, devotion, Scripture, art, and prayer.

- *Jesus at the Center of My Messy Life: Tales from the Next Step Community*

The team of authors at community.findmynextstep.org share their stories and insights in refreshing ways that help you take a next step.

Find out more at www.findmynextstep.org.

Key Concept Calendar, Days 1–7

<table>
<tr><td>1</td><td></td><td></td><td>2</td></tr>
<tr><td>3</td><td></td><td></td><td>4</td></tr>
<tr><td>5</td><td></td><td></td><td>6</td></tr>
<tr><td>7</td><td></td><td>*Renewal: The Spirit conforms us to Jesus and his death and resurrection.*</td><td></td></tr>
</table>

Key Concept Calendar, Days 8–14

8

9

141

10

11

12

13

14

Spiritual Warfare: The Spirit conforms us to Jesus and his testing in wilderness and Garden.

Key Concept Calendar, Days 15–21

15

16

17

18

19

20

21

*Pouring:
The Spirit
conforms us to
Jesus and his
overflowing
service to others.*

Key Concept Calendar, Days 22–28

<table>
<tr><td>22</td><td></td></tr>
<tr><td></td><td>23</td></tr>
<tr><td>24</td><td></td></tr>
<tr><td></td><td>25</td></tr>
<tr><td>26</td><td></td></tr>
<tr><td></td><td>27</td></tr>
<tr><td>28</td><td></td></tr>
</table>

Hospitality: The Spirit conforms us to Jesus and his heart for the outsider and marginalized.

Key Concept Calendar, Days 29–35

29			30
31			32
33			34
35		*Rhythm: The Spirit conforms us to Jesus and his rhythm of life in the Spirit.*	

About Visual Faith™ Ministry

The Key Concept Calendar and Secret Code Prayer experiments in this book were adapted from standard Visual Faith™ Ministry tools and techniques. The Ripple Prayer and the Filled Up and Overflowing faith experiment were created specifically for Next Step Press using insights developed by Visual Faith™ Ministry.

Visual Faith™ Ministry is the collaborative effort of online and "in-real-life" learning communities to enrich, encourage and enable the vital connections between visual and kinesthetic learning styles and the storytelling of God's faithfulness in our lives.

Visual faith is reading, reflecting, and responding to God's Word. It welcomes writing, drawing, designs, and color to create reminders of faith that help tell the story for followers of Jesus. Visual faith reminds us that we are made in the image of a creative God.

Visual faith honors God's creative sanctification of believers on a daily basis and is the basic process of bringing together our great gifts of prayer and God's Word. It adds visual, kinesthetic, and tactile adaptations that make meaning for us in our daily lives. Visual faith is a "selfie" of our time with God, helping us to remember, retain, and be ready to share it with others.

In all of these ways and more, Visual Faith™ Ministry helps to answer the question, "What does this mean for me?"

Find more Visual Faith™ Ministry resources at
www.visualfaithmin.org.

More from Justin Rossow

You, Follow Me, Volume 1: Advent and Christmas
(Next Step Press, 2019)

The first of the daily discipleship travel logs from Next Step Press, Volume 1 includes readings, devotions, and faith experiments to help you prepare for following Jesus at Christmas and into the New Year.

Preaching Metaphor: How to Shape Sermons that Shape People (Next Step Press, 2020)

The lenses we use to understand and reason about our lives and our faith have a profound effect on the way we live and believe. Justin Rossow turns decades of pulpit experience and PhD-level metaphor theory to create a practical and engaging help for teachers and preachers.

More from Leopoldo A. Sánchez M.

Sculptor Spirit: Models of Sanctification from Spirit Christology (IVP Academic, 2019)

The rich and varied research in this study from Leopoldo Sánchez creates a fertile seedbed for faithful reflection on the Holy Spirit. By engaging theologians across time and around the world, *Sculptor Spirit* provides a rich dialogue with real benefit to the way we read Scripture and understand the Spirit's work in our own lives.

SDG